THE SURVIVOR'S GUIDE TO LIBRARY RESEARCH

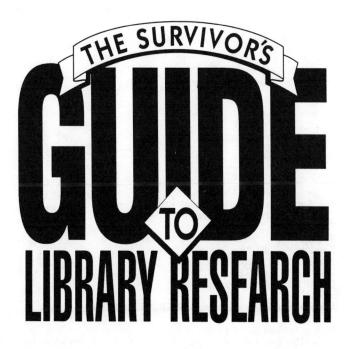

THE SURVIVOR'S GUIDE TO LIBRARY RESEARCH

WILLIAM B. BADKE

ZondervanPublishingHouse
Academic and Professional Books
Grand Rapids, Michigan

A Division of HarperCollins*Publishers*

The Survivor's Guide to Library Research
Copyright © 1990 by William B. Badke

Requests for information should be addressed to:
Zondervan Publishing House
Academic and Professional Books
1415 Lake Drive S.E.
Grand Rapids, Michigan 49506

Library of Congress Cataloging-in-Publication Data

Badke, William B., 1949-
    The survivor's guide to library research : a simple, systematic
approach to using the library and writing research papers / William
B. Badke.
        p.   cm.
    ISBN 0-310-53111-X
    1. Libraries and readers–Handbooks, manuals, etc. 2. Libraries
and students–Handbooks, manuals, etc. 3. Bibliography-
-Methodology–Handbooks, manuals, etc. 4. Research–Methodology-
-Handbooks, manuals, etc. 5. Report writing–Handbooks, manuals,
etc.   I. Title.
    Z710.B23   1990
    020'.72–dc20   90-42264
                                                                          CIP

Edited by Susan T. Lutz and Ed van der Maas
Designed by Committee, H. Winfield Tutte, Chair

Printed in the United States of America

90 91 92 93 94 95 / CH / 10 9 8 7 6 5 4 3 2 1

To my wife
Rosemary
and to my children
Shawn and Jordan
who have supported me all the way

Contents

PART III.   DOING BATTLE

Read This First

"Why should I read a book on research method anyway? I get by in libraries. I get passing grades on papers."

True, you do get passing grades, but you would be happier with A's and B's. You get by, but probably with a lot of needless suffering.

When I introduced a course in library research to my students not long ago, I described the common sight of students wandering hesitantly into the library and roving desperately up and down rows of books, inwardly pleading that a title relevant to their subject would jump out at them.

I was interrupted by an aggrieved voice asking, "Sir, have you been following me?" I had not, but I have watched many others. Day by day as I observe students muddling through time-consuming "research," I wish I could lead each one by the hand and say, "Here is a better way. Walk ye in it." This book is my attempt to do just that.

Recent studies have shown that most college and university students experience anxiety when approaching a library. The main reason seems to be that most college students, even most graduate students, have no idea how to plan a systematic strategy for library research. The result is wasted time—time that could have been spent researching the four other papers due next week; missed bibliography items that were crucial and could have meant a better grade; and an overall slovenliness that would move a hobo to tears of envy and makes the reasearch that *was* done look careless and incomplete.

Approach what is to follow with an open mind. This book is intended to help you, and these methods have had proven success. Here is what you will get from careful adherence to the strategy outlined in this book:

- Faster research
- More comprehensive research

READ THIS FIRST

- Better bibliographies
- Fewer careless errors that require rechecking
- **Better grades**

So relax. Abandon your prejudices. Surprisingly, you might even enjoy this.

About the Dingbats

A dingbat, in addition to a "nitwit" or "kook," is a typographical symbol or ornament.

In this book different dingbats identify sections that need special emphasis or that need to be set apart in some way:

☞ highlights instructional hints for the reader;

■ highlights lists of information;

● highlights lists of advantages, reasons, or cautions.

In addition, three horizontal solid squares, ■■■, identify information that is not quite distinct enough to be put into a list but nevertheless needs special attention. The same thing applies to three horizontal open circles, ○○○. Here the material does not need to be put into a list of advantages, reasons, or cautions, but does need to be highlighted more than the text around it.

PART I

Basic Training

1

Taking Charge

Many of you reading this book may be saying to yourselves, "I do not have a good essay in me."

My response is, "Of course you don't. A good essay is primarily out there. You have to find it, appropriate it, and make it your own."

Now, before you run off to lurk in a dark alley frequented by black market essay-sellers, let me offer you an ethical alternative. What follows is a list of the basic things you need to get the information that is out there and effectively turn it into a paper of your own.

1. You need an intense desire to write a *good* paper, not just an average one. By definition most people can write an average paper.

2. You need to take your time and plan your research as a *strategy* rather than as a mad dash through the book stacks. Libraries know when you have reached the panic stage. The books close ranks and refuse to be found. Titles in the catalog trade places so that you can't locate them. The smell of musty books renders you numb and silly.
   Don't panic, whatever you do. Take it easy. Work out a plan and show these gatherings of the printed page who's in charge.

3. To do that, you need to *develop lateral thinking.* Lateral thinking is akin to what happens in a football game: The quarterback has no openings at all. If he moves with the ball, he'll be flattened. So instead of moving forward, he throws the ball sideways to another player who can move it forward. The steps are obvious:

- Recognize that your advance along one line is blocked.

- Abandon your approach and look for another one.

- Run with your new approach and make it work.

Moving from the playing field back to the library, here is how lateral thinking can be used in research. All too often, students stop looking when the catalog reveals nothing on their assigned subject or when they can't find a certain reference book. But *no strategy can afford to be so rigid that it can't change direction when it dead-ends at a brick wall.* That's when your research strategy needs a good lateral. The next section will show you *when* you need to use lateral thinking and *how* to think that way.

Recognize When Your Line of Research is Blocked

"I am writing a paper on the Lollards. I don't know who they are or were (and I'm finding it hard to care). When I'm done— if I can find anything in this obviously undersized library—I will have a paper describing the Lollards. It will stress description of the Lollards. Its theme will be 'Describing the Lollards.' The point I will seek to make is that the Lollards can indeed be described."

Exciting, isn't it? Even before you start you know that those old Lollards are going to thrill you to pieces—if, that is, you can get one to stand still long enough to be described.

No, it isn't exciting. It's just another paper—sigh—just as tedious as the last one you had to write.

But ask a professor, any professor. He or she will tell you that professors are not strangers to boredom. In fact, the most tedious thing professors do is mark your essays. Let's face it: Most students write dull papers. They bore their professors and their professors pay them back by giving them C's.

It is forgivable to make mistakes occasionally, even to be late turning in a paper (if your dog died and you broke your leg in three places all on the same day).

But it is unforgivable to bore your professors. **It is even more unforgivable to bore yourself.**

Look for Another Approach

This leads me to the first principle of good lateral thinking:

Never Accept a Topic as Given

Where do professors get these strange topics anyway? Either the topic is so general that you have no idea how to tackle it ("The Lollards") or so detailed in a twisted sort of way that you know you will never find enough material on it to make a decent essay ("The Influence of the Lollards on Twentieth-Century Education in the South"). For the latter type of topic there is not much hope, but fortunately most assigned topics are of the former variety.

Let's face it. Most professors loathe the thought of reading another student paper on the Lollards. Their unspoken plea is, "Say something *new*."

So here is the strategy: Find out some details about your topic (chapter 3 shows you how to do this) and then give the topic a sharp "neck-twist." Go to your professor and say politely, "Would you mind if I pursued *this* approach to the Lollards? It really looks interesting."

Your professor's heart will turn to mush and he or she will say solemnly, "Yes, all right," while inside he or she is shouting, "A new approach! I'm getting a new approach!"

- Caution: Do not ever say, "May I write on the Albigenses instead?" This tells your professor that you do not like the Lollards, and you most certainly will end up writing on the Lollards anyway.

Make the Topic Viable

What is this 'neck-twist' you need to perform on your topic? There are two simple steps: (1) narrow your topic, and (2) put your own slant on it.

First, how do we *narrow a topic*? One of the biggest reasons why so many essays do not work is that the topic is too broad. Take the Lollards. (Please!) To cover the Lollards, you will have to find out who they were, what they believed, where they lived, when they lived, and what happened to them. It's too much. If a professor has given you "The Lollards" as your topic, choose one aspect and concentrate on it.

For example, you might do an introductory two pages defining them and stating the main events of their existence. Then you could concentrate the balance of the paper on their beliefs. Or you could introduce them and their beliefs but concentrate the bulk of your paper on the events of their rise, flourishing, and fall.

A little later (in chapter 3) we will be looking at quick research that can define the boundaries of your topic by finding its major subdivisions. But for now, recognize that any topic can have several aspects or approaches. Take the subject "Abortion." This can be dealt with from the perspective of a number of disciplines:

- *Medicine:* How are abortions performed? Is a fetus a real person from a medical standpoint?

- *Law:* What are the laws on abortion and how are they being interpreted?

- *Philosophy:* How do we define personhood? Is a fetus a person?

- *Ethics:* What are the main ethical issues surrounding abortion, and how are these debated?

- *Psychology:* Is the argument about the psychological health of the mother a key consideration? What are the psychological aftereffects in women who have had abortions?

- *Religion:* How valid is the argument against abortion as proposed by Catholics and evangelical Protestants? How do proponents of other religions view the debate?

- *Sociology:* Is it true that women have reproductive rights? Is the concept behind the slogan "Every child a wanted child" valid? Are there reasonable alternatives to abortion (care homes, private adoption agencies, etc.)?

We have broken down our overly broad topic by academic discipline and have come up with a list of narrower topics under the general heading "Abortion." There may be other ways to limit topics. For example, a paper on Joseph Conrad's novel *Lord Jim* could be narrowed to "Jim's Personal Conflicts as the Key to the Theme of Conrad's *Lord Jim*." (I got an A+ for that one in an undergraduate English course). Similarly, "Problems of Youth in Modern Society" could become "Youth in the Midst of the Sexual Revolution" (notice how that allows you to focus on just one problem youth face today).

Whatever the topic, you can usually narrow it. In general, when you get an assignment, assume that your topic is too broad until you can prove to yourself that it is not.

Then, *put your own slant on it.*Most research papers are descriptive rather than analytical. Let me clarify: *Description* explains what is out there. *Analysis* also explains what is out there but goes a step further and places some kind of judgment or evaluation on the facts: *Why* is what's out there out there? Is it good that it is out there? Is it bad? Could what is out there improve?

Run With Your New Approach and Make It Work

Once you have narrowed your topic and put your own slant on it, you are ready to throw your literary lateral pass. That is, you are ready to turn your research into an original, well-organized essay. Here are some examples of how it is done:

"The Thought of Erasmus of Rotterdam"

Your much-beloved philosophy professor has assigned you "The Thought of Erasmus of Rotterdam." Having perused a few reference sources, you narrow your topic to "The Humanism of Erasmus of Rotterdam." You could, at this point, decide to begin your paper with "Erasmus of Rotterdam was born in the year . . . " You *could* go on to explain his teaching on humanism and then conclude, "As is clear from the above, Erasmus was an important person who deserves more attention."

This method is also called "regurgitating your sources." It establishes a conduit between the books you read and your writing hand without ever really engaging your brain. It also makes for a very dull paper.

On the other hand, you could be analytical. Having read your sources and affixed the details firmly in your mind, you could engage your brain and do something exciting. How about contrasting the humanism of Erasmus with the teaching of the modern "Humanist Manifestos I and II"? This would involve studying Erasmus but would go on to demonstrate the differences between early humanism and the modern variety.

Now you have the makings of an approach that could contribute something fresh and exciting to the

19

topic. Your professor might even remember reading it when you ask about it later.

"Homelessness in Our Cities"

You are taking a sociology class and are supposed to write a paper on "Homelessness in Our Cities." You could regurgitate some statistics, recite a few case studies and conclude, "It is obvious that we need to take action on this issue." Or you might narrow and "neck-twist" your topic to "The Debate over Solutions to Homelessness in our Cities." As you did your research, you could then weigh the merits of the various proposed solutions and then pit them against one another.

"The Causes of the Ecological Crisis"

For a course in ecology, you have been assigned "The Causes of the Ecological Crisis." You narrow this to focus on human values in society as causes for the crisis.

A descriptive paper could string together quotations from current leaders in the debate who are decrying our wastefulness and greed. You could conclude, "Thus it is clear that we must change our attitudes." You have narrowed your topic, but not put your own slant on it.

An analytical paper would go further, perhaps with a critique of the common view that the Western Protestant ethic, with its desire for dominion over the earth, is at the heart of the trouble we are in. Your topic could be, "Is Protestantism Responsible for the Environmental Crisis?" Your analysis would defend your personal judgment on the facts you have uncovered.

"Behaviorism as a Model for the Social Sciences"

> Your subject is the impossibly broad "Behaviorism as a Model for the Social Sciences." You have narrowed it down to the social science model presented by behaviorist B. F. Skinner. You might take the easy way and write a descriptive paper—an extended summary of Skinner's book *Walden Two* (but easy is the way that leads to destruction).
>
> Instead, why not be cunningly analytical by arguing that the social science model in *Walden Two* is flawed because it fails to take human depravity sufficiently into account (a common problem with behaviorism)?

One final note of caution: Always clear your narrowed down, "neck-twisted" topic with your professor before you begin. Disaster could be awaiting if you do not—some professors do not like surprises.

2

A User's Guide to the Library

Most students believe that the best way to approach the library is with full body armor and drawn sword. Libraries are threatening places for many reasons:

- Everybody in them knows more than you do.

- You can't find the catalog (and when you find it you don't know what to do with it).

- You can't find the entrance to the library stack maze.

The real reason, of course, why libraries are so threatening is that it is so hard to see the forest for the trees. There are too many books on too many subjects for a person who wants only a few books on one subject. You literally need a road map just to find your way around.

Somewhere within those walls is exactly what you need, but you get the feeling that first you will have to sift through everything you *don't* need. Fortunately, libraries are set up to help you get to the right place with reasonable haste. Three facets of the library are there to help you.

The Classification System

Even though you are probably sure that classification numbers follow some inscrutable logic of their own, designed to confuse you, they can really help. The primary role of any classification system is to group books on similar subjects together.

There are two basic systems in use in North America: the

Dewey Decimal Classification System and the *Library of Congress Classification System.* They do similar things but follow quite different patterns.

■ ■ ■

The *Dewey Decimal System* uses three-digit numbers from 000 to 999. Each group of 100 numbers refers to a different broad discipline. For example, 100–199 is philosophy, 200–299 is religion, 300–399 is social sciences, and so on. Within each discipline there are subdivisions, often broken down into tens. For example, within the religion class (200–299), 220–229 is Bible and 230-239 is theology.

The numbers within these subdivisions (221, 222, etc.) are further subdivisions, and *further* subdivisions of these subdivisions are indicated by decimals (hence the name Dewey Decimal System). For example, within the history subdivision related to the ancient world (930), 933 is the history of ancient Israel, while 937 is reserved for Roman history. Roman history is further subdivided into periods. For example, 937.01 relates to the earliest period and 937.02 relates to the Roman Republic, ca. 500–31 B.C., and so on.

The only way to keep your head in the Dewey system jungle is to remember the broader disciplines you are working in and recognize, for example, that your 937.02 for the Roman Republic is within the 937 number for Roman history, which is part of 930 (history of the ancient world), which in turn is part of the history and geography classification (the 900's).

Call numbers for both the Dewey Decimal System and the Library of Congress system often conclude with a letter, a number, and a date, in this form:

910.7
.D37
1990

The .D37 is a "cutter number." Its purpose is to identify the book *you* want and distinguish it from the 147 other books that have the 910.7 number. When you reach the 910.7 section in the library, simply read the cutter numbers on the books *alphabetically* until you get to the D's and then look for .D37. The date can help you decide if the book is current enough for you. It can also distinguish between two books both labelled .D37, one published in 1986 and one in 1990.

■ ■ ■

The *Library of Congress System* uses letters (one or two) and short numbers. The letters indicate the broad disciplines and the numbers stand for the subdivisions within those disciplines. In this scheme, numbers following the letters often do not go beyond four digits.

With the Library of Congress system, the pattern of broad subject, subdivision of that subject, and subdivision of the subdivision is, unfortunately, not as obvious as in the Dewey system. For example, DG77 and DG78 deal with aspects of Roman civilization, while DG81 and following deal with Roman history. (In Dewey, by contrast, Roman civilization is under a totally different number than Roman history).

Part of the difficulty is that major subjects do not actually have their own number from which subdivisions can be made. In the Library of Congress tables of classification numbers, Roman history is a heading with no number. There are only numbers for subdivisions, and a simple transition from DG78 to DG81 shifts you without warning from one subject to another. Thus you will have to be careful that you know just where you are.

Library of Congress "cutter" numbers follow this sort of format:

LT
7040
.B52
1990

But with the Library of Congress system , there may be two cutter numbers, the second acting as a subdivision of the first:

LT
7040
.B52L27
1990

■■■

Is one system better than the other? That depends. Dewey is used in many libraries with fewer than 100,000 volumes (and in some libraries with far more). Most larger libraries and many smaller ones prefer Library of Congress, because Dewey numbers in subdivisions can get unacceptably long.

The advantage of Dewey is that it is a relatively simple system to understand and use. The Library of Congress system is more complicated for most students, since it uses both letters and numbers, and its method of subdivision is not obvious. But it has the advantage of easy subdivision without long numbers.

The fact is that you will have to learn to live with one or the other of these systems, and maybe even both, during your student days. Get to know the main features and quirks of your particular system. It is a small investment in time that will pay dividends throughout your college career.

- One note of caution: Not all the books on any one subject will be found under the same classification number. It depends on how your subject is treated.

For example, if you are writing on responses to the suicide crisis (why did that topic come to mind just now?), books on suicide as an ethical issue will appear under a different classification number than books that deal with society's response to the problem. For suicide in crisis-counseling situations, still another number will be used. It all depends on the approach taken to the subject. That is why a classification scheme by itself is not a sure-fire means of access to what you really want in a library. In fact, though it is often the first approach a student will try, it is probably the least reliable if you want comprehensive information.

The Reference Collection

While the classification system enables you to focus on specific areas of the library rather than having to wander through all of it, the reference collection is a sort of mini-library within the larger library. It generally covers all the major subjects covered in the larger library, but it does so by means of dictionaries, handbooks, guides, subject bibliographies, and so on. It is organized in exactly the same way as the main library. Thus, in a library that uses the Dewey system, the reference collection will have books from 000 to 999. It is a library in miniature of books that cannot be checked out of the library. Because it is smaller, it can provide you with good clues as to how to approach the larger loan collection.

Sad to say, many students bypass the reference collection entirely. After all, who wants a silly three-page article on the Lollards when there are whole books out there just waiting to be devoured? By the time you finish reading the next chapter, I trust that you will withdraw that question and realize that the reference collection may well be the gateway to the best paper you have ever written on the Lollards or any other subject.

For now, I want you to understand that the reference collection, a mini-library within the library, is an excellent means of approaching the whole collection with something less than the terror you usually experience. Take some time to wander through it and look at the titles and classification numbers. Just browsing will allow you to see how the whole library is set up. It will show you where your subject fits into the scheme of things. Once you begin actually using it, you will find that it is a treasure trove of good information.

The Catalog

In our technological age, a library catalog can come in many forms, from cards to microfiche to online computer terminal. But whatever the format, the library catalog is your index to the collection. As such, it is probably your best means to gain access to the information you want.

There is hardly a student who does not at some time despise the catalog more than Cain despised Abel. This is tragic, because the catalog, like the classification system and reference collection, is there to help you. Unfortunately, frustration seems to abound whenever it is used. Let me try to eliminate some of the confusion.

A library catalog usually has three types of access points (things to look up):

authors,
titles, and
subjects.

In some libraries, the author, title, and subject entries are intermixed (a "dictionary catalog"). Other libraries combine authors and titles but keep subject separate or even split authors from titles from subjects ("divided catalogs").

Authors and titles are generally not much of a problem. It helps, of course, if you know the alphabet, but at your sophisticated level this is obviously no problem. If you can look up a name in a telephone book, you can generally use an author or title catalog with relative ease.

Subject catalogs are tougher to master, however, and offer almost limitless opportunities for growth and development. The reason for this should be plain. If I point to a chair and say to you, "Name this object," you will first check me over to see if I am missing any brain cells and then respond, "A chair." But if I say, "*Describe* this object in one phrase," you will experience more of a problem—and your description will almost certainly not be identical to someone else's.

The same is true of books. If I say, "Name this book," you could answer, *"New Perspectives on the Ecology of Rain Forests"*.

26

The accepted heading ➤

See also this heading (sa) ➤
This heading is not accepted (x) ➤
Same as "See also" (xx) ➤

Subdivision of "Abortion" ➤
(i.e. Abortion — Law and legislation)

Further subdivisions ➤
(i.e. Abortion — Religious aspects
— Protestant churches

Abortion *(Indirect) (Birth control, HQ767-767.7; Medical jurisprudence, RA1067; Obstetrical operations, RG734; Obstetrics, RG648)*

sa Abortifacients
x Feticide
xx Birth control
    Fetus, Death of the
    Infanticide
    Obstetrics
    Pregnancy, Unwanted
— Complications and sequelae
— Law and legislation *(Indirect)*
xx Offenses against the person
    Sex and law
— Religious aspects
— — Catholic Church *(HQ767.3)*
    x Catholic Church and abortion
    xx Church and social problems
— — Catholic Church, [Coptic Church, etc.]
— — Protestant churches *(HQ767.3)*
    x Protestant churches and abortion
    xx Church and social problems

But if I say: "Describe this book in one phrase," you might suggest, "Rain Forests—Ecology," or "Ecology—Rain Forests," or something else. Notice that each of these descriptions, if used as a subject heading, would wind up in a different place in an alphabetical listing of subjects.

Subject headings are not obvious because they involve judgment rather than simple labeling. Thus the use of the subject catalog can be a real problem. May I suggest a strategy?

☞ Think of key terms or phrases that could describe your subject, and write them down.

☞ If your library has a copy of *Library of Congress Subject Headings* (we will call this work *LCSH*), haul it out and use it. This massive set lists the standardized subject headings used, not only by the Library of Congress, but by most North American libraries. Thus you can look up your tentative subjects and see whether or not these are in standard use. Even if they are not, *LCSH* often tells you what to look up instead. Unfortunately, just as I have built up your hopes, I have to splash cold water on you—*LCSH* is not that straightforward and easy to use. Figure 2-1 shows how LCSH works.

☞ If you do not have access to *LCSH*, you will have to try out your tentative subject headings directly in your library's catalog. Depending on how many or how few cross references are provided, this will be either a rewarding or a dismaying procedure.

☞ Look up your subject(s) in your library's catalog. If you find nothing, try a related subject or two. If you still find nothing, ask your librarian for help.

☞ If you have located some items in the catalog, be sure you write down the full call numbers—the letters and/or numbers the book is classified by (see pages 00–00). The path from the catalog to the library stacks is the Road of Great Forgetfulness. From this point it should be a simple matter to round up the titles you have spotted in the catalog.

Chances are, of course, that these items will already have been signed out by someone else, but don't lose heart. You can cajole your classmates into sharing or you can place a hold on a book if you've allowed enough time for research. Also your librarian can usually find a few more items than you or your friends were able to dredge up—so ask.

We have seen three ways to approach the library: the classification system, the reference collection, and the catalog. Now we are ready to begin looking at an overall strategy for locating the books and periodicals so necessary for transforming your paper from a turkey to an eagle.

A Note on Entering Bibliographical Data

This short section is for those of you who have no idea how you will list in your bibliography the books and periodicals you find. Now is the time to learn this, because you will need to write down the relevant information *as you do your research* (that is, while you still have the book and before your friend Joe takes it along on a ski weekend).

Your school has, no doubt, provided you with some sort of handbook telling you how to record the information which describes a book or periodical article. Let me add a few pointers:

☞ Take your handbook seriously. Yes, your professors really do care that you list the place of publication before the name of the publisher, and that you use a colon instead of a comma.

☞ For most items there are essentially five things you need to record:
author
title
place
publisher
date
Memorize these. Turn them into a song. Do whatever you have to, but make sure you always remember to record at least this much.

☞ For the purposes of note taking, you will also have to record page numbers for information you gather. More on this in a later chapter.

☞ Articles in reference books can present a problem. Look at the end of the article to see if an author's name or initials are listed. If initials are given, there will be a section somewhere in the book that provides the full name. The format demanded by your school may require you to begin the entry with the author of the article, not the editor of the

29

reference book. The article title will probably be given with quotation marks around it. Check in your school's handbook for the proper order and punctuation demanded.

☞ Periodical articles call for a bibliography entry style all their own. Have a close look at your school's handbook.

Again, always take care to record the right information about the book or article you are researching *while you are researching it*. More information on note taking and related matters will be provided in Chapter Eight.

For more details on the two main approaches to citing information, see the Appendix.

PART II
Master Plan

3

How to Decide What You Need...and Find It

In the last chapter we considered three methods for approaching the library. Any one of them could be the first step in your strategy to snare the sources you really want. But one of the three—the reference collection—is the best starting point in most cases.

The Reference Collection

Start here. If you don't know the reference collection too well, you can use the catalog in one of two ways to locate the reference sources you want.

☞ Look up your subject in the subject catalog and write down the classification number used most often. Find the reference collection.

☞ Look up your subject and find a card with the subheading "Dictionaries."

Reference books, when you locate them, will generally appear in the form of dictionaries or encyclopedias on general or specific topics. As well, handbooks, atlases—in fact, any tool that involves looking up brief information—may be found in the reference collection.

Call numbers for reference books often have at the top the designation "R" or "Ref." or "REF." Some libraries use no special designation on the call number but print reference call numbers on a label with a different color (e.g., regular books might have white spine labels but reference books have pink ones).

Here's what you are looking for: a work on your subject that deals with your specific topic in three pages or less.

I'm already cringing at the thought of your reaction: "Three pages? I need a *book* on the subject. **A BIG FAT BOOK. TEN OF THEM!**"

Do you know what I say to students when they tell me that they want a big book on some subject or other? I say, "No, you don't." When their shock dies down, I am able to show them that starting small is beautiful and starting big is depressing.

Why would you want three pages or less instead of five hundred?

- You want to get a handle on your subject right away. If you don't know who the Albigenses were, a big book will smother you in so much detail that you could spend hours just finding basic facts. Let's face it: you don't need this kind of recipe for depression.
  A short article will quickly set the scene for you, answering the five W's of intelligent inquiry: who, what, when, where, and why. Without basic knowledge to build on, you will find most larger works (which assume you have basic knowledge) incomprehensible.

- You want to know the area your subject covers and what its major divisions are. Until you can see what approaches are commonly taken to the subject, what boundaries and divisions it possesses, you will flounder.

- You want to know how your topic fits into the larger discipline, especially if you suspect that your library may have limited resources on your narrow, neck-twisted topic. If you know, for example, that the Albigenses were people from a certain period of Christian church history, you can look for information on them in more general church histories or dictionaries of the Christian church. Thus, even if there are no books specifically on your topic in the library, knowing what discipline your topic belongs to can lead you to works which contain vital information for your paper.

- You want a list of some of the standard works on your topic. Many reference sources also include bibliographies at the ends of their articles, and you can usually be sure that the works listed there are standard works.

Related to this is the fact that the author of a reference article is often a recognized authority in the field. (Remember: He or she will usually be indicated by initials at the end of the article. You can find the full name in the reference work's abbreviation dictionary.) Try looking up the author's name in your library's catalog to see if the author has written a book or two on the subject.

Let me illustrate the value of approaching your research through reference sources. You've been dying to know who the Lollards were (admit it). Since I suspect that they belong to church history, I check out a couple of dictionaries of the Christian church and discover:

WHO?

The Lollards were followers of John Wycliffe; more generally, the term was used later of any serious critic of the church. Key figures in the movement were Nicholas of Hereford, William Swinderby, and John Purvey.

WHAT?

Their doctrines, summed up in the Twelve Conclusions (1395), included personal faith, divine election, and the Scriptures as the sole authority in religion. They demanded that every person enjoy the individual right to read and interpret the Bible.

WHERE?

The movement existed in England and Scotland primarily.

WHEN?

The movement began in the 1380s (A.D.) and went underground after 1431 due to persecution. It declined in the mid-1400s but revived about 1490. It figured prominently in the congregational dissent of the seventeenth century and the rise of the Hussites in Bohemia.

WHY?

Its claim was that it was a reaction to the control over human life and spirituality exercised by the Catholic Church.

My two reference sources (*Oxford Dictionary of the Christian Church* and *New International Dictionary of the Christian Church*) also yielded between them a bibliography of thirteen sources on the Lollards.

Have I convinced you? Use reference works first. That way, you will have your basic facts straight before you wade into the big stuff.

The Preliminary Outline

You now have enough basic data to begin thinking through the approach you want to take to the paper. We've already looked at the ways to narrow down and "neck-twist" a topic. The time has come to begin outlining it.

Take note of the fact that your outline at this point will usually be desperately preliminary. But it is a start, and you will be able to use it as the basis for a growing structure which, by the end of your research, should be at least a full-blown skeleton. Here are the steps:

1. Whittle the theme of your paper down to a sentence or two.

2. Look at the key words or subtopics in your theme and use these as outline headings.

3. Arrange the headings into some sort of logical sequence if possible (you may have to go for another cup of coffee before this is possible).

4. Give your outline time to hatch and grow up. Research essays are like baby birds. They only begin to squawk and finally to fly after they've grown for awhile. You need to let the embryonic paper outline in your cranium hatch and begin to mature, the cells shuffling and reshuffling as you think of what to say, how to say it, and in what order.

From this time on, your preliminary outline will be a part of you, growing and changing as you research. Keep it ever before you in your sitting down and your rising up.

(For a more detailed discussion of outlining, see Chapter 10).

Mining Gold from the Catalog

We librarians suffer a great deal. Everyone thinks we're stuffy. Some think we're inherently lacking in the higher intellectual gifts. And no matter how much we try to help you, you continue to ignore most of the bounty we have prepared. Nowhere is this more true than in the library catalog.

Once you have gotten a handle on your subject and have started an outline, you will want to proceed to the catalog to see if you can locate more works on your topic. Perhaps you have some titles from the bibliographies in your reference sources. Or more likely, you are going to try a subject approach.

Let me show you how to dig gold from catalog entries. In the following figure you will find copies of three catalog card entries—author, title, and subject cards. We will look at elements of these entries in turn, to see how they can help you narrow your search and come up with clues to other important works on your subject.

Authors

If an author has one book on your subject, he or she may have written others which could also be relevant. Look up the author in the catalog to see what else may be available under the author's name.

301.58 Lewis, I. M.
.L48   Ecstatic religion; an anthropological study of spirit
1971   possession and shamanism / [by] I.M. Lewis. —
        Harmondsworth, Eng. : Penguin Books, [1971].

        221 p. ; ill. ; 19 cm. (Pelican anthropology library
        Bibliography: p. [207]–211.
        ISBN 0-14-021227-9
        1. Ecstacy. 2. Spirit possession. 3. Religion and
        sociology. I. Title.

BL626.L48   301.5/8
                       75-26289

Ecstatic religion

301.58 Lewis, I. M.
.L48   Ecstatic religion; an anthropological study of spirit
1971   possession and shamanism / [by] I.M. Lewis. —
        Harmondsworth, Eng. : Penguin Books, [1971].

        221 p. ; ill. ; 19 cm. (Pelican anthropology library
        Bibliography: p. [207]–211.
        ISBN 0-14-021227-9
        1. Ecstacy. 2. Spirit possession. 3. Religion and
        sociology. I. Title.

BL626.L48   301.5/8
                       75-26289

ECSTACY

301.58 Lewis, I. M.
.L48   Ecstatic religion; an anthropological study of spirit
1971   possession and shamanism / [by] I.M. Lewis. —
        Harmondsworth, Eng. : Penguin Books, [1971].

        221 p. ; ill. ; 19 cm. (Pelican anthropology library
        Bibliography: p. [207]–211.
        ISBN 0-14-021227-9
        1. Ecstacy. 2. Spirit possession. 3. Religion and
        sociology. I. Title.

BL626.L48   301.5/8
                       75-26289

Titles

Have you ever been so desperate, or so confused, that you used the title catalog like a subject catalog? This is the ultimate horror to many librarians: A student chooses a key word related to his or her subject and looks up the word in the title catalog, hoping that there will be a book beginning with that word.

As a librarian, I dare not advocate this approach openly. But strange as it may seem, it actually works sometimes. Take the title card above: *Ecstatic Religion: an Anthropological Study of Spirit Possession and Shamanism.* If you were actually studying "Shamanism" you could look it up as the first term in a possible title. You might find: Eliade, Mircea. *Shamanism: Archaic Techniques of Ecstasy.*

With a manual catalog (card or microfiche), such searching for title key words is a task that could label you as a bumpkin or an extremely desperate student totally out of resources. Yet strangely, this method has now achieved respectability in computer catalogs. If your title is accessible on an online terminal, you may be able to search for title key words, not just at the beginning of the title, but at any position in the title or subtitle.

Publication Information

If you are a beginning student, you probably don't know a Baker from a Harper & Row from a Zondervan. But as time goes on, you may spot certain publishers who typically handle certain kinds of topics well or take certain approaches. Thus a publisher can be a clue to the value of the book you are considering.

The date of publication is also relevant. If you are doing a paper on "Current Issues in Euthanasia," you probably won't want a book published in 1932. If, however, you are doing "A History of the Euthanasia Debate," that 1932 book may be a very useful primary source.

Collation

Coll-what? Collation. That's the descriptive material in the middle of a catalog entry, such as the number of pages and physical height of the book (in centimeters). Useless, you say? Not really. The number of pages in a book may tell how deeply the author has gone into the subject. A small book on a broad topic will be pretty skimpy. On the other hand, a long book on a narrow topic may be more than you want.

Watch as well for the abbreviations "illus." or "ill." These mean "illustrated." Now I know you're too old for picture books, but illustrations in a book on ecstatic religion may help you picture more clearly the nature of ecstatic religious rites.

Series Title

This is found in parentheses right after the collation if, indeed, the book is part of a series. More and more books these days are being published as parts of ongoing series. Why? Partly to organize material into subject or discipline groupings. But mostly, if the truth can be told, so that publishers can sell more books. If you've bought one book in a series and liked it, chances are that you will buy others.

Why am I being so frank? Simply because the money-making angle of series can at times mean that knowledge of a series title will be of no help to you. To the extent to which a series title indicates a subject grouping of books, it can lead you to other books which may also be relevant to your topic. Some series titles, however, serve more to sell books than to delineate a subject. In those cases the series title may be meaningless, or the series may include books on such a wide range of subjects that the chances of finding another book on the same topic within the series are negligible.

In our example, looking up other items in the "Pelican Anthropology Library" will probably not give us much help, since anthropology is probably too broad a subject field to produce other works on ecstatic religion. Even so, it might be worth trying. If you want to do so, just look up the series title as you would look up any title.

(Take note that there will be a separate catalog entry for each volume in the series. You may have to look at a number of entries in a row before you find your item.)

Indication of Bibliography

In research, a cardinal rule is to use each item you find to help locate other items on the topic. Thus you need to watch for a note, following the collation and series title, which indicates that the book contains references to other works.

Here are some common formats for such notes:

"Bibliography: p. 207–211." This tells you that the book has one bibliography section, though it may also have useful footnotes throughout.

"Includes bibliographies." This indicates that there are several bibliography sections in the book, often at the end of each chapter.

"Includes bibliographical references." This means that there is no bibliography as such, but there are citations to other works in footnotes.

Subject Tracings

At the bottom of a catalog entry you will find one or more subject tracings, each of which follows an Arabic numeral. These tracings indicate all of the subject headings under which that book has been cataloged. For example, Lewis' book (see catalog records, p.00) could be found under "Ecstasy," "Spirit Possession," or "Religion and Sociology" in the subject catalog.

Why is more than one subject used? Partly it is to help a library user who might approach a topic from one of several possible directions. Also, books that cover subjects in an interwoven fashion will need several subject headings. Finally, interdisciplinary works, which operate in dead zones between two or more subjects (disciplines) need more than one subject heading.

Note: Subject headings are not generally given for portions of books. You will not be provided with a separate heading for the subject of a single chapter, only for topics covered in the book as a whole or in a substantial portion of it.

What can you do with subject tracings? They are often clues to related subjects you might also consider looking up. For example, if you are studying "Trance States in Animistic Religion" (fun topic) and have discovered the subject "Ecstasy," the tracings for Lewis' book (see catalog records above) might give you a clue to look up "Spirit Possession" as well.

Call Numbers

The call number is provided in the upper left corner of the entry. It tells you, of course, where in the sequence of library shelving the book is located. You can do two basic things with this information from the catalog:

MASTER PLAN

1. Go to that area of the library and browse for more items. Remember that many call numbers represent subdivisions of broader subjects. Thus you should look at both the specific call number area and the area for broader numbers in the sequence, where you may find more general works that contain chapters or sections on your topic.

2. Find a relevant subject, look it up in the catalog, and write down the call number listed on each successive entry for that subject.

"But won't they all have the same call number?" you ask innocently. Sad to say, they may not. It depends on the way in which the subject is treated. Lewis' book (see catalog records, p.00) is a good example. In the Dewey system it is classed in the social sciences (300's) because the topic is dealt with from a sociological standpoint. But it could as easily have been found in the 290's were it to be handled as a religious topic or from the standpoint of belief systems.

Armed with a few call numbers from the subject catalog, you can go to those areas of the library and browse for more books.

4

Stalking the Elusive Reference

You've done it. You've searched the reference sources and wrung every last bit of information from the catalog. Now, triumphant for the moment, you walk off with three photocopied reference articles and four books. At this point you see yourself as amply prepared to write a fifteen-page article on the basis of seven sources. You might even get a passing grade.

But there is so much more that you could have found. "Not a chance," you retort. "If it's not in the catalog, it's not in the library. I have purged the collection of everything on my topic." No, you haven't. There are at least three more possible book searches, not to mention the periodical literature.

Books as Bibliography Sources

You are used to seeing a book as a source of information in the form of wise and scholarly words on your topic. But a book can also be a rich source of another kind of information— references to other books and articles used or recommended by the author.

Here is a strategy that could net you a whole host of materials:

☞ Find a recent book (one to five years old) on your topic. If there is no such thing in your library, find a recent reference article with a bibliography.

☞ Take note of its footnotes and/or bibliography and write down a citation for anything that looks relevant to your topic.

☞ Here's the potentially tricky part, so light up a
few more brain cells: Find some of the items you
have jotted down in step 2. (These may be books
or articles). Open them and look at *their* footnotes
and bibliographies.

☞ Jot down these further items, locate them, and
carry on the procedure until you wear yourself
out.

Let's try an example.

I am doing a paper on British scholar C. S. Lewis. When I
look up his name in the subject catalog, I discover that the
rather small library I am using has only three books on him,
and two of these have been signed out. Is my problem simply
that very little has been written about Lewis? It might help me
to know the answer to that question before I trek twenty miles
across town to another library. Also, it would be good to have a
list of a few standard titles in hand before I go.

The one book I have located is David Barrett, *C. S. Lewis and
His World* (1987). In its bibliography I find listed the following
titles:

Humphrey Carpenter, *The Inklings* (1978).

Jocelyn Gibb, ed., *Light on C. S. Lewis* (1965).

R. l. Green and Walter Hooper, *C. S. Lewis: A Biography*
(1974).

John Peters, *C. S. Lewis: The Man and His Achievement*
(1985).

Chad Walsh, *The Literary Legacy of C. S. Lewis* (1979).

The day I make the journey across town to the other library,
it is raining (inevitably). I take my soggy list and locate the book
by John Peters, *C. S. Lewis: The Man and his Achievement*. It has
no bibliography, but its endnotes reveal the following:

Humphrey Carpenter, *The Inklings* (1978).

Jocelyn Gibb, ed., *Light on C. S. Lewis* (1965).

Carolyn Keefe, ed., *C. S. Lewis: Speaker and Teacher* (1971).

W. L. White, *Images of Man in C. S. Lewis* (1970).

The first two were also listed in the first book I searched. I
decide to try to locate the book by Humphrey Carpenter.
Unfortunately, Carpenter is hiding and cannot be found. So I
choose the next most recent book, the one edited by Carolyn
Keefe: *C. S. Lewis: Speaker and Teacher* (1971). Its endnotes
provide extensive information on Lewis's own works, particu-

larly those which began as lectures. There are citations to reviews of these works as well.

My book bibliography search has paid off. Not only do I have more books, but I have data on some of Lewis's more obscure works, along with information on where to find reviews of them.

You could continue the process indefinitely, depending on how broad your library's resources are, how many items you need, and how exhausted you are beginning to feel. But eventually one of two things would happen:

You may find that the bibliographies begin to refer to books that are very old and are thus either unavailable or not relevant (depending on the subject). Notice that we see a rough progression in our searches above from newer to older materials.

Or you may begin to see repeat citations. We have already found this with Carpenter, who seems to be on everybody's list. When you do see repeats, you know either that you have located the most important works on the topic or that you have locked into one particular approach to the topic, and all the writers taking that approach are citing only one another. Watch for this latter problem. You may have missed other relevant approaches.

Why go through this kind of exercise at all? Looking at the titles of the items we found, we could say that most of them would be easily accessed by looking up "Lewis, C. S. (Clive Staples), 1898–1963" in the subject catalog. This is true, and if you want only a few items, the catalog may serve your purposes admirably. But if you want more, there are three reasons why a book bibliography search will be helpful:

- Bibliographies tend to reveal which works are considered to be the more important ones.

- It is entirely possible that some works you spot in a book bibliography may be under a subject heading or classification number that for one reason or another is different from that for other books on your subject.

- Bibliographic citations, especially when they are in footnotes, can often tell you what position the cited work takes on the topic.

Now that you are convinced, I hope, that this approach can help you, you might wonder why you should search the subject catalog at all. Why not just find your sources through book bibliographies? There are two good reasons:

First, no writer is obligated to cite all the good books on a topic. Thus you may miss some very relevant material.

Second, authors can cite only those works available to them when they were writing. For more recent materials, you will have to use the library catalog. For example, Kathryn Lindskoog's *The C. S. Lewis Hoax* (1988) might be a useful, though rather unusual, addition to our bibliography. It was published after all of the books found in our book bibliography search on page 00.

Thus I recommend that you use both methods. Depending on the topic, one may pay off more richly than the other. But both have their unique contributions to make.

Finding Articles in Edited Books

When librarians provide subject headings for a book, they generally cover only the main subjects for the book as a whole or for a major portion of it. This creates a real problem when you find a book called: *This and That: Essays in Honor of Horace Q. Blowhard* (a made-up title, but very real in principle).

Buried in this gem may well be a specialized article on your topic. But the only way you will find it, in many cases, is by seeing a reference to it in some other source. Only when all the articles in the collection are related to the same topic (e.g., *Essays on Abortion*) do you have any real hope of locating them reliably.

It was thus almost inevitable that someone would come up with a subject index to articles in edited books (an edited book is a collection of essays by many scholars brought together under one cover by an editor). It is called *Essay and General Literature Index* and provides year by year volumes of subject indexing to such articles, so that you can locate an essay on the sociological implications of the revival of the yo-yo craze within the book to honor Horace Q. Blowhard. Of course, this index cannot hope to cover every edited book. But it does pretty well all the same.

In the subject of religion, there is a specialized source to do the same thing: *Religion Index Two* (published by the American Theological Library Association).

Subject Bibliographies

In some instances, careful people who love minute detail have produced whole volumes of bibliographies in specialized subject areas. If there is one for your subject, you may well have one of the best tools for finding more items on your topic. You can locate such a bibliography by looking up your subject area in the subject catalog of your library and seeing if you can locate the subheading "Bibliography." Some libraries actually group all their bibliographies in one area for quick access.

Subject bibliographies come in a variety of formats. The most useful provide a survey of the topic and then annotate each bibliography entry, usually arranging entries under appropriate subdivisions of the subject. For example, you might find Warren S. Kissinger's *The Parables of Jesus: A History of Interpretation and Bibliography* (Metuchen: Scarecrow, 1979). This gives you a brief introduction to current research, and then provides a 230-page, detailed history of interpretation before turning to a bibliography divided into such subtopics as "Parables in General," "The Barren Fig Tree," "Blind Leading the Blind," and so on. While the bibliography itself is not annotated (an annotation is a comment telling you about the content and/or worth of the bibliography item listed), the introductory and historical materials provide rich background.

A related form of good bibliography is the "research guide," which is either an annotated bibliography subdivided by subtopics, or a series of "bibliographical essays" which describe the subject area by referring to and describing key works in the field. The bibliographic essay can be very valuable to you because of the amount of information it gives on each work it cites.

From this point, we leave the good and move into the bad and the ugly. Here we have the bibliography that is not subdivided or provides no annotations. While it may be better than nothing, it can use up a lot of your valuable time while you try to find what you want. At least it will give you a splendid opportunity for growth and development (should you desire another one).

Take note, as well, of the fact that periodical articles often provide state-of-the-art subject bibliographies, citing the most current research. By the end of the next chapter, you will know how to locate such articles.

There is one drawback with most published subject bibliographies. They are dated. If a completed book manuscript takes six months to two years to be published, it is already somewhat out of date. By the time it has been sitting on the library shelf for five years, it is really becoming a fossil. Thus specialized bibliographies are generally best for picking up the standard works of the past.

o O o

One strong tool to help you locate more recent books and articles which provide bibliographies is *Bibliographic Index*, an annual publication which you can search by subject. If you want books and articles containing bibliographies on crisis counseling, you can look up "crisis counseling" and find exactly what you need.

In this chapter we have been looking primarily at how to find items in book literature. We now move into those challenging (and dreaded?) periodicals.

5

Making Your Way Through the Periodical Maze

Even thinking of using periodicals in an essay may produce in you a shudder of horror. You imagine sitting down before piles of journals or magazines, thumbing through each one in an anguished quest for something (anything!) on the "The Implications of Max Weber's Approach to the Sociology of Cities." Hours later, in bitter defeat, you will emerge, red-eyed, with one article which is only vaguely relevant.

Periodical searching used to be done that way when your grandfather was a wee lad in school. Now things are very different, due to the rise of periodical indexes.

Periodical indexes are just that—they are subject indexes to articles in selected periodicals. With them, you can zero in on relevant articles in minutes rather than in hours. Here's how they are produced:

Each year, a number of indexers sit down before piles of periodicals (spaced out over the year, of course) and assign subject headings to each article. These in turn are entered into computers which, in due course, produce subject indexes in book form. Often such indexes come first in paper-bound fragments (monthly, quarterly, or twice per year). This, of course, makes them very current but forces the researcher to look up the same thing in several issues.

As a courtesy to the users, therefore, most indexes *cumulate* every year or two. This means that the databases are reorganized so that all of those fragmentary issues are combined into one volume in such a way that you only have to look up your subject once. (The computer databases are saved for another purpose in many instances, but we'll get to that in the next chapter.)

Thus each volume of a periodical index covers a predetermined list of periodicals over a set period of time (usually one to two years), providing subject access to individual articles in those periodicals. The kind of subject access varies. Some indexes use Library of Congress Subject Headings while others create their own systems. This means that the term you use to describe your subject may produce great results in one index but yield nothing in another, because a different term is used there. This is another opportunity to use the skill you developed earlier: thinking of many different ways to describe your topic, and checking the periodical index under those alternative listings.

Periodical indexes may also feed you other goodies—author indexes with abstracts of articles, book review indexes, and even information on new books in the field.

In the following pages, we will look at a number of these indexes. Your own library may not have all of these, or may have others which I do not mention. Not to worry; the key is to learn how to use periodical indexes in general. Thus you will become handy with whatever one(s) may be found in your own library.

Learning to Use a Periodical Index

Before we attempt to list some of the more prominent indexes in the humanities and social sciences, we'll use one example to show how to use periodical indexes in general. For our purposes, *Religion Index One* contains many standard features and will serve as our model.

Religion Index One is the largest and best of the periodical indexes in religion. It originally came out in 1949 under the title *Index to Religious Periodical Literature* and, as it grew up, it changed into *Religion Index One* (as of the 1977–78 issue). Its little sister is *Religion Index Two*, which we encountered in the last chapter. (Remember? Articles in edited books? If not, you need to do some reviewing.)

Religion Index One, up to the end of 1985, had three major sections: a subject index to articles, an author index with abstracts, and a book review index. (Prior to the 1975–76 volume, there was no author index with abstracts.) As of 1986, however, things have changed. Now *Religion Index One* is just a subject index to articles. The author index with abstracts has been discontinued and the book review index is now separately published as *Index to Book Reviews in Religion*.

A subject index is relatively easy to understand (though less easy to use), but let's look more deeply first at the purpose for the other two parts.

The author index with abstracts (deceased as of 1986, R.I.P.) had two basic purposes. First, it gave author access to articles. If, for example, you know that a certain author was prominent in your subject area, you could use this part of the volume to find out quickly what articles he or she had produced in a particular year. If you knew of an article by someone but lacked full bibliographical information, you could look it up under that person's name.

Second, the author index with abstracts provided abstracts to some of the articles listed. An abstract is basically a summary telling you what the article covers and concludes. Thus, if you found an article listed in the subject index that looked like it might be useful, but you were not sure it was worth finding, you could locate an abstract to see if it covered what you wanted. In addition, an abstract is a great help in deciphering the main arguments of articles that are complex and hard to follow. When we list some of the common indexing tools later in this chapter, you will notice that a number of them contain abstracts.

The book review index section (as of 1986 a separate publication called *Index to Book Reviews in Religion*) provides information as to which issue of which periodical contains a review of a certain book. For example, you might want to see what scholars thought of the work by Joe Padowski, *The Church Choir Director's Hiring-Firing Book* (made-up title). You would look up "Padowski, Joe" in the book review index. Underneath the entry would be listed citations to one or more reviews of the book, along with the information needed to locate those reviews in their respective periodicals.

Why would you want to see a book review? I can think of at least four reasons.

- First, the book may take a novel approach. You will want to know if other scholars liked it.

- Second, you may have to review the book yourself for a course assignment. While you would never dream of plagiarizing another person's review, it would be helpful to know that most people hated the book before you write a review full of glowing praise (it is hard to wash egg off your face).

- Third, you may want some quick information on the main contents and arguments of a book before you wade into it yourself. A review will usually give you that information.

- Fourth, at times a review will serve as an article in its own right. If the reviewer is a key scholar in the field, the review may provide valuable further information on the subject as the reviewer debates with the book being reviewed.

- Caution: Books are often not reviewed extensively until they have been on the market for one to three years. Thus, for a 1988 book, your best results would be found in indexes for 1989–1990.

Back to *Religion Index One's* subject index section. First, let me give you some tips on deciding what subject heading you will look for:

☞ Start as specifically as possible. This means that if you are dealing with the Holy Spirit, you will look up "Holy Spirit," not some broader term like "Theology."

☞ Only if a narrow search reveals too few references (or none at all) should you choose a broader term.

☞ One peculiarity of subjects is that they often come in pairs. Take, for example, "The Influence of Lollard Thought on Education in the South." (You thought I'd forgotten about the Lollards— surprise!) This is really a two-part subject. You have the Lollards (remember that any name, including "Lollards," can serve as a subject heading) and you have Education. This leaves you with two possible approaches by subject: "Lollards" and "Education."

You need to make a decision as to which subject area would probably give you the most articles listed. But—pay attention!—*you then pursue the* other *subject area.* Why would you want to do that? Let me answer your question with another question: Have you ever had to look through three two-column pages of small print subject index material under a broad heading like "Education," when all you wanted to find was one small reference to Lollards in some article? If you choose the subject area which is *least* likely to have a lot of entries in it, it is far easier to spot a reference to the other area (in our case, looking up "Lollards" to see if any of the articles refer to education in connection with the Lollards).

☞ Don't give up if one volume of a periodical index yields little under a perfectly good subject heading. Remember that indexes come out every year or two. It may be that your particular topic was not as hot an issue among scholars in one year as it was in another. These things go in cycles. Try an index for another year. Make sure, of course, that your subject heading really is used by that index.

☞ Be prepared for frustration and take it philosophically. No, you are not stupid. No, your index is not stupid. It's just that you and your index sometimes have communication problems. Get that lateral thinking out and find another way to make the index work better for you. It you're prepared for potential setbacks, you won't get so emotional when they happen.

The format of *Religion Index One* (henceforth *RIO*) is quite typical of periodical indexes, and that is why we are using it for our extended example. Let's go through a couple of specific searches:

"The Apostle Paul's Use of 'Body' to Refer to the Church"

I am writing on the Apostle Paul's use of the term "body" to refer to the church. Notice the two-part nature of this subject: I have "Paul" and I have "Body." I suspect that the larger number of entries will be under "Paul", so I look up "Body" instead, starting with the more recent volumes of *RIO* and working back in time.

When I look up "Body," I immediately see that there are several subheadings. Searching down through these, I find the heading that I feel is closest to the topic: "Body, Human—Religious Aspects–Christianity." Here's a facsimile of that section:

To my joyful wonder I discover that the third item down is an article entitled "The Church as the 'Body of Christ': A Pauline Analogy." Even better, it has a bibliography in it (did you notice the "[bibliog.]" after the book title?), which should lead me to other relevant works.

MASTER PLAN

BODY, HUMAN - RELIGIOUS ASPECTS - CHRISTIANITY
    The body of your father [ancestors in Melanesian
       Christianity] Gresch, Patrick F. <u>Point</u> [6] No. 1
       178-185 1977.
    The body spiritual. Elkins, Thomas <u>Chr</u> <u>T</u> 29 No. 13,
       24 S 20 1985.
    The church as the 'body of Christ': a Pauline
       analogy [bibliog.] Breed, James L. <u>Th</u> <u>R</u> <u>(Near</u>
       <u>East)</u> 6 No. 2, 9-32 1985.
    Food for thought: maintaining the temple [fitness
       and nutrition]. <u>Fund</u> <u>J</u> 2 No. 9, 28-31 O 1983.

I have located only one item, so I write down all the relevant information and then decide to try "Paul" as a subject heading. After a bit of rumbling around headings and subheadings, I find "Paul, Saint, Apostle–Theology–Church." Here is what is under the heading:

PAUL, SAINT, APOSTLE - THEOLOGY - CHURCH

    Accountability without bondage: shepherd leadership
      in the biblical church [table]. Troxel, A. Burge.
      <u>J</u> <u>Chr</u> <u>Ed</u> <u>(US)</u> 2 No. 2, 19-26 1982.
    The church as the 'Body of Christ': A Pauline
      analogy [bibliog.]. Breed, James L. <u>Th</u> <u>R</u> <u>(Near</u>
      <u>East)</u> 6 No. 2, 9-32 1985.
    Contending for the faith or just contentious [St.
      Paul]. Keener, Nelson. <u>Fund</u> <u>J</u> 2 No. 8, 68 S
      1983.

I notice that I am now looking at various topics related to Paul's doctrine of the church in general. Because "Paul" was conveniently subdivided, there were not as many entries to look at as I feared. The second of these again gives me James Breed's article.

But how do I know that the article by Breed takes the approach that I want? Since this is the 1985 edition of *RIO*, it still has the author index with abstracts section. Going to this part of the volume, and looking up "Breed, James L.," I find a handy little abstract that tells me what I need to know:

BREED, James L. The church as the 'body of Christ':
    a Pauline analogy [bibliog.]. <u>Th</u> <u>R</u> <u>(Near</u> <u>East)</u> 6
    No. 2, 9-32 1985.
    This article presents an exegesis of several key
    passages in the Pauline NT corpus where he treats
    the concept of the 'Body of Christ', to see how
    he uses this as the basis for his understanding
    of the relationship between Christ and the church.

The actual abstract is a bit longer than this, but I hope

you get the idea of what such an abstract can do for you.

In this case it tells me that I want this article. I want it so badly that I would kill or maim for it. *I must have this article!* (Either I am trying to liven up a dull page, or I am paraphrasing a desperate student in the heat of the research moment.) The next step is to find out what journal the article is in. My citation calls it *"Th R (Near East)."* Very helpful. Now I must go to the front pages of the volume and find an abbreviation index. This reveals that *"Th R (Near East)"* is *Theological Review.*

The moment of truth has come. You have a citation to an article on your topic. Does your library have the article? You want the journal *Theological Review*, volume 6, issue number 2, pages 9–32. If your library has a catalog of its own periodical holdings, consult that. If not, find out from your librarian how specific issues of journals can be located.

Be sure you find out what format your material is in. A number of libraries are now heavily into microfiche or (shudder) microfilm, especially for back issues. Librarians know what you think of micro formats, but they are a good way to compact whole issues of journals into a fraction of their original size. Please exercise maturity and be enormously thankful that the article is available to you, regardless of format. Later, as your eyes go bloodshot and weepy while you read off a glaring screen, you can be grateful for yet another opportunity for growth and development.

If your library does not have the item you want (which often happens—sigh—because these indexes cover hundreds of journals), your library may have a catalog of periodicals in other libraries in your area. If you cannot locate the article at all, do not get unduly upset. There are more volumes of *RIO* which you can search through, and more articles to find. (But if you are desperate to have this particular article, a company called University Microfilms can run you off a copy of many things for a price. Ask your librarian about this service. Alternatively, the article may be available through interlibrary loan.)

Now locate your item and enjoy.

Those steps again in brief:

- Having chosen a subject, look it up in your periodical index.

- Try other possible headings if needed.

- Check out the author index and abstracts, if present.

- Check the abbreviation index to get the full name of the journal.

- See if your library has that issue of that journal.

- Locate your item and enjoy.

"The Writing of History in Ancient Times"

This time I want to see a book review of John van Seeters' *In Search of History: Historiography in the Ancient World and the Origins of Biblical History* (1983). I am doing a paper on the writing of history in ancient times (was biblical history writing different?, etc.), and I have heard that van Seeters is a key, though controversial, work. Is he right? Is this work respected? A review or two will tell me and might give me some alternative viewpoints on the issue.

I go to *RIO's* book review index section in the 1983–1984 volume and find seven reviews listed, each giving me the information I need to locate them in the journal issues in which they are found. The 1985 volume lists six reviews. The 1986 separately published index yields a scattering more. Obviously, before I even begin, I can see that the book has sparked considerable comment.

Here is a facsimile of the entry for the 1985 volume, just so that you an see how such reviews are listed:

```
Van Seters, John. In Search of History:
 Historiography in the Ancient World and the
 Origins of Biblical History. Yale Univ. Pr, 1983.
 Halpern, Baruch. J B L 104,505-509 S 85.
 Kaiser, Otto. Z Altt W 96 No 3,464-465 1984.
 Petersen, David L. C B Q 47,336-340 Ap 85.
 Smith, Morton. J A A R 53,133 Mr 85.
 Walters, Stanley. S R 13 No.4,495 1984.
 Zevit, Ziony. A S O R Bul No. 260,71-82 Fall 1985.
```

The first item (Halpern) tells me that there is a

review of van Seeters in *Journal of Biblical Literature* (full name of journal gained from abbreviation index). The volume number is 104, the issue I want was published September 1985, and the page numbers on which I will find the review are pages 505–509.

From this point I need only follow steps 4 to 6 of our first search to locate actual reviews.

Common Index and Abstract Tools

With the wide variety of indexing tools published, it is of value to list the more common ones in the social sciences and humanities, and to describe some of them:

Reader's Guide to Periodical Literature

This is a useful general index, popular with many undergraduates who want quick information from a broad range of the more common journals and magazines.

Biography Index

An index to books and periodical articles devoted to the famous and the less-than-famous. If your essay relates to a person, this is a valuable guide.

Humanities Index

Another general index, originally part of *Social Science and Humanities Index*. This tool covers all the subjects normally found in the humanities division in a college or university (English, history, philosophy fine arts, and so on).

Social Sciences Index

The second part of the original *Social Sciences and Humanities Index*. It is devoted to social sciences (psychology, sociology, economics, politics, etc.).

Art Index

Contains articles on the fine arts.

Business Periodical Index

Covers periodicals devoted to finance, administration, industry, economics, etc.

Education Index

Devoted to educational periodicals for all levels of education, preschool to university. Includes some yearbooks and monographs.

Current Geographical Publications

Deals with geographical periodicals, books, government documents, pamphlets, and maps.

Historical Abstracts.

Covers periodical literature that specializes in history. Includes abstracts.

Philosopher's Index

Subject index plus author index to all major philosophy periodicals in several languages; with abstracts.

Psychological Abstracts

Covers a vast array of periodicals directly or indirectly related to every branch of psychology. Note that this and the next tool have abstracts.

Sociological Abstracts

Deals with a broad range of sociological periodicals.

Several Book Reviewing Tools:

Book Review Digest

Contains actual excerpts from book reviews.

Book Review Index

A good general source (no excerpts).

Index to Book Reviews in the Humanities

An index to reviews of books in the broad discipline of the humanities: art, literature, history, philosophy, etc.

Index to Book Reviews in Religion

An index to book reviews in religious periodicals.

Excursus: Further Indexes in Religion

The religion field, mysterious to many students, has spawned a goodly number of specialized indexes to help you deal with its enormous amount of literature. If you are working on a religion-oriented paper, the following may help you:

Christian Periodical Index

This index, which began coverage with 1956, provides subject access to a select number of evangelical journals and magazines, unlike *Religion Index One (RIO)*, which covers journals of many doctrinal stances, including evangelical journals. Use *Christian Periodical Index* (henceforth *CPI*) as a first source for subjects of special interest to evangelicals or for research when you are writing brief papers. Use it as a backup source (after *RIO*) for larger projects or for projects where you might want coverage of more evangelical journals than *RIO* handles.

CPI has a combined author and subject index (no abstracts) plus an index to book and media reviews.

Guide to Social Science and Religion in Periodical Literature

You may not like the long title, but this index (which began coverage with 1970) is a valuable source for articles that relate to the social sciences and religion. The social sciences, of course, include subjects like psychology, sociology, current social issues, economics, law, and so on. This index covers both religious and non-religious journals, making its scope usefully broad.

With *Guide to Social Science and Religion in Periodical Literature* you have only subject access, and here is where the problems begin. To be honest, this index can be pretty difficult to use (are you listening, publishers?). It majors on broad headings with subdivisions.

Thus, if you want an article on the problems of pastors' wives, you do not look up "Pastor' Wives" or "Ministers' Wives" or "Clergy Wives" or even "Wives of Pastors." You look up "Ministry, The" and search for the subheading "The Minister's Wife." If you can get past this ongoing difficulty, this index can be a useful tool.

Elenchus of Biblica

This is too much. Not only are you already having problems figuring out periodical indexes, but now I throw you a Latin one. This index began as part of the journal *Biblica*, but since 1968 it has been published in large separate annual volumes. While it is heavy going for the beginning student, it contains a wealth of material on biblical subjects as well as biblical theology. The citations include many languages, but quite a few relate to English articles. This index even covers a number of books in key subject areas.

The older volumes of *Elenchus* have headings in Latin, but take heart: the newer issues have English headings. The real problem lies in the confusing array of headings and subheadings. How will you ever find what you want?

May I suggest the indexes at the end of each volume? There are very good author, Greek and Hebrew word, and Scripture indexes. Scripture indexing, in particular, can be very helpful. Do you want an article on the theological problem in Hebrews 6? Just look up Hebrews 6 in the Scripture index, and the appropriate article(s) will leap out at you.

Notice that each reference (citation) to a book or article in *Elenchus* is numbered. The indexes at the back of the volume point you to citation numbers, not pages. This is a pattern found in quite a few periodical indexes. Notice as well that *Elenchus* usually comes out about two years after the publications it cites. Oh well, you can't have everything.

Religious and Theological Abstracts

This is a quarterly journal filled with abstracts of periodical articles. It has four major headings: Biblical, Theological, Historical, and Practical, with subdivisions for each heading. Even though it appears small at first, this tool covers well over 200 religious periodicals. Its major advantage lies with the fact that abstracts are provided. With the demise of the author index with abstracts in *Religion Index One,* this fills the gap quite well. It certainly helps if you can see the basic nature of an article before you hunt it up and spend time reading it.

There are two potential drawbacks. First, the main heading/subdivision approach makes it difficult to find the right section quickly. Second, the index does not cumulate (That is, it does not combine the information in all four issues so that you need only look up a heading once). These problems are nicely offset by the fact that the final issue in each volume contains a handy set of indexes to the whole volume. Thus you will have difficulties only with the current year's issues until the final one comes out. This tool has served students well since 1958 and deserves greater recognition.

New Testament Abstracts and *Old Testament Abstracts*

These two publications, each of which appears three times per year, can be treated together since they do the same task. The New Testament version first appeared in 1956, and the Old Testament in 1978.

The basic aim of these two works is to provide abstracts of periodical articles related to the Bible. They cover each book of their respective Testaments, as well as citing articles on biblical topics in general, including biblical theology. The Old Testament version also covers inter-testamental and apocryphal books. Both tools boost user-friendliness markedly by providing, in the last issue of each volume, a good set of indexes to the whole volume.

An added feature of both of these tools is the book notices section, a series of abstracts of recent books related to biblical studies, divided by subject. One further help provided with *New Testament Abstracts* is a one-volume index to the first fifteen volumes published.

MASTER PLAN

Missionalia

Missions education is a growing discipline in Christian colleges and seminaries, and the amount of research material available is large. *Missionalia*, a journal published three times per year, includes in each issue a major section entitled "Missiological Abstracts."

This is subdivided by main headings and subheadings, which can make it a bit difficult to use. The coverage, however, is very good, and an index to the headings is found on the back cover. *Missionalia's* abstracts also cover articles in edited books, making it an additionally valuable resource.

The ATLA Indexes

ATLA, for the uninitiated who thought it stood for All Thinkers Love Anchovies, is the American Theological Library Association, the producer of *Religion Index One* and *Religion Index Two*. In recent years, ATLA has been putting together specialized subject indexes in religion.

The advantage of these indexes, beyond the obvious one that each focuses on a specific subject, lies in the breadth of their coverage. They include material from all of *Religion Index One*, *Religion Index Two*, and *Research in Ministry* (an index of Doctor of Ministry projects, begun in 1981).

The list of these specialized indexes is growing. While many small libraries cannot afford too many of them, you may find a few in your library's collection.

6

Exotic Resources for the Adventurous Researcher

Besides the meat-and-potato sources of information for research, there are also more exotic dishes for the adventurous or the desperate. I never quite know where to put these. (If I were a mechanic, I am sure that I would always have a spare bucket of parts left beside the car after I finished rebuilding the engine.) Thus a chapter of odds and ends lurks before you.

If my bucket of extras looks foreign to you, or neither your library nor any other nearby has the materials or capabilities I am about to describe, I will (sigh) understand if you skip to the next chapter. You have my permission. But there could be some good help here, even for a term paper. If you are doing a large project or a thesis, this chapter is a must, and my permission to skip it is rescinded.

Citation Indexes

The citation index is a child of the computer. As such, it can do things which no other kind of periodical index can do. There are three such indexes in existence, all produced by the same company. The *Arts and Humanities Citation Index* covers works which we could describe as "liberal arts"—literature, philosophy, religion, history, music, painting, and so on. There is also a *Social Sciences Citation Index* (psychology, sociology, anthropology, economics, politics, law, etc.), and a *Science Citation Index*.

MASTER PLAN

What do they do? Before you can understand that, you need to know how they are organized. There are three parts:

Source Index

Here is what a typical entry will look like:

```
DAVIS WT*
   COMPETING VIEWS OF THE KINGDOM OF GOD
                    IN AFRICA
   ECUMEN REV      32(2):115-128            80      5 R
       UNIV IBADAN, DEPT RELIGIOUS STUDIES,
                IBADAN, NIGERIA
   BIBLE                  ISAIAH                    55
   AJAYIFA            65  CHRISTIAN MISSIONS
   FOSTERCARTER A     74  SOC DEV
   FRANK AG           66  MONTHLY REV            17 17
   WARREN M           65  MISSIONARY MOVEMENT
```

This section is the easiest of the three to understand. The producers of the citation index have looked at over 1000 journals and have arranged an index, in alphabetical order by author, of all the articles in these journals. Under each entry are then listed all the works cited in the footnotes and/or bibliography of that article.

In our example, the article is by W. T. Davis and is entitled "Competing Views of the Kingdom of God in Africa." We are then given information on where the article is located and some background on the author. Following are the five items this article referred to in its footnotes and/or bibliography, including one reference to the Bible. The numbers before the titles refer to the year of publication. The numbers after refer to the volume and page number if given in the original article.

At least two valuable kinds of searches can be made with a source index. First, if you know a certain writer has been working in a subject area, you can look up that person's name in the source index. There you will find listed the articles he or she has written for the period covered by the source index volume you are looking at.

Second, if you find a reference to a key article but cannot get access to that article, the source index will at least tell you what works that article included in its footnotes and bibliography. Thus the source index can be a good means for increasing the bibliography for your paper.

Citation Index

It looks like this:

```
AYANDELE EA ..................................................
    ED ELITE NIGERIAN SO 1974
        COPLEY A    J IMP COM H              7   128  79
        DAVIS WT    ECUMEN REV              32   115  80
    MISSIONARY IMPACT MO 1966
        COPLEY A    J IMP COM H              7   128  79
```

Confusing? Let's first look at what a citation index does, and then we'll try to decipher the above entry.

Concentrate. The citation index is a sort of reverse source index. It tells you who referred to a certain book or article in their own periodical article. First you get a heading for a certain author and subheadings for that author's works. Then underneath you have references to periodical articles which referred to the work in the heading.

In our example, the author in the heading is E. A. Ayandele. The works of his which are listed are "Ed Elite Nigerian So" (abbreviated title) and "Missionary Impact Mo" (which stands for *Missionary Impact on Modern Nigeria, 1942–1914*). In the case of the former work, two periodical articles referred to it: one by A. Copley and one by W. T. Davis. In the case of the latter work by Ayandele, the same article by A. Copley made a reference to it. The citation index will allow you enough information to be able to locate the periodical articles that referred to Ayandele's works.

Two valuable functions are performed by this index. First, if you have a book or article on your subject but you want more recent materials, you can look up the book or article (by author's name) and see which articles have referred to it. Articles that refer to your item will obviously have been published more recently and are often on the same or a related topic.

Second, if you read a book or article that takes a new approach or appears controversial, you can look it up in the citation index to see who has referred to it. Finding these articles in turn could lead you to a rich source of comment on the work you are considering. The very number of citations can tell you whether or not the work is even producing comment.

Permuterm Subject Index

This strange name is a combination of "permute" (to arrange in all possible ways) and "term." The index looks like this:

```
BALLET
    ALIGNMENT ....................................NICHOLS L
    CURRENT ........................................GEITEL K
    DANCERS .......................................WILLIAMS P
    GERMANY .......................................KOEGLER H
```

This is a subject index comprised, primarily, of key terms from the titles of periodicals. It allows you to pair any two key terms. Remember that subjects often come in pairs?

If, for example, you wanted to find an article on "current trends in ballet," you could look up "Ballet" as in the above entry, and find ranged below it the word "Current." Opposite "current" you would find that there is an article with "ballet" and "current" in its title. The article is by K. Geitel. If you now look up Geitel in the Source Index, you will find all the details by which you can locate the article.

The citation indexes do have drawbacks. For one thing, they are very costly. Thus many libraries cannot afford them (though grant programs are available). As well, they are complicated to use. Finally, they appear each year and so have the same problem as periodical indexes—you may have to do the same search in a number of volumes to find what you want.

Still, they can be a valuable resource. I see them as a bridge between the conventional periodical indexes and computer databases.

Dissertation Indexes

Some of the most exciting work being done in academia is found in dissertations produced by masters and doctoral students in seminaries and universities. While you may not often want to go to the trouble of searching out this material, it can have real value. There are two major sources for information and access to theses and dissertations.

Dissertation Abstracts International

This is a subject catalog of doctoral dissertations. Produced by University Microfilms International, it is a link to thousands of dissertations which UMI has available for sale (in paper or microfiche format). Since colleges or universities with large collections of dissertations in their own holdings are rare, you will probably have to (gulp) buy the dissertations you need. And they are not cheap. (A better alternative may be to request them through interlibrary loan).

Dissertation Abstracts International (DAI) comes in two sections: Section A (Humanities and Social Sciences) and Section B (Sciences and Engineering). Each section provides subject access, an author index, plus an abstract of on average 350 words for each entry so that you can see what each dissertation covers.

If you want to order a dissertation for purchase, the key is the code number appearing to the lower right of the bibliographic information about the thesis. Give this, plus author/title information, to your librarian, who should be able to help you order it.

DAI is now available on compact disk so that libraries of the future (and some of the present) will offer you the capability of searching the index like this by computer.

TREN

No, this is not a movie about people who live inside a computer. This is the Theological Research Exchange Network, a comparative newcomer in supplying theses in religion on microfiche.

TREN invites seminaries to send them masters theses, which are then microfiched (usually on one to three fiches). An annual catalog is produced, and the theses are available for sale at quite low prices compared to UMI.

This is a growing resource which should prove useful as its collection grows. Check with your librarian on this one.

ERIC

First we had TREN, now ERIC. Obviously this is not the ferocious offensive tackle of some college football team. In fact, it is the Educational Resources Information Center, a U. S.

67

government-sponsored collection coordination agency for reports and articles in education.

Because education is a broad discipline, many of the items have value for people not even interested in education as such. For example, there are ERIC reports on counseling handicapped and gifted children, Bible college and seminary functions, libraries, and linguistics.

The key to finding ERIC material is *Research in Education*, an index providing subject and author access to the collection. Unlike dissertations, libraries which have the index are also provided with the reports themselves, usually on microfiche. One drawback lies in the fact that subject headings used in *Research in Education* are not standard. Thus you may have to use the *Thesaurus of ERIC Descriptors*, an index to the headings used in ERIC, which, though confusing (what isn't these days?), can be of help. ERIC can also be searched by computer link to its database.

Computers in the Library

This is the computer generation, and I would not dream of insulting you by asking whether or not you are technology literate. Of course you are. But in order for you to communicate more effectively with your parents, let me share a simple definition: A computer is a machine that arranges and rearranges information. As one of my library school professors put it, a computer is a "fast clerk."

Computers in libraries are a relatively new phenomenon, and we are seeing only the beginning of what could be. First, however, let me get one thing out of the way. I am constantly being asked, "When are you going to put your library on computer?", meaning, "When am I going to be able to read the full text of any book right off the screen?"

My answer is, "If you mean every book in the library or even a large number of the books—NEVER." While the advent of the compact disk for computers (you're probably familiar with music CDs) allows for an incredible amount of storage, it is not economically feasible to put most books onto disks. Nor do readers want to mess up their eyes reading off a screen all day long. (With dread I imagine myself eating these words fifteen years from now.)

What, then, is available for computers in libraries?

Databases

For quite some time libraries have been able to interface (through a modem) with bibliographic databases. You may be saying, "Whoa. Back up a bit." Let me illustrate with an example. Imagine all of *Religion Index One* loaded into a computer so that you could type in "Baptism" and get, printed on the screen, all of the citations to baptism listed in *RIO* since 1949.

You can, in fact, now do that through a modem telephone link between a library's computer and a database. But your quick mind is already moving ahead and you say, "But I've got the printed version of *RIO*. I don't need a computer."

There are real advantages to using a computer for searching, especially because computers have dramatically increased search capability.

Search capability is a complicated issue. Let me try to simplify it. I can only give you here the basics of what is involved. First, here's another term to add to your list: "Boolean Logic." Boolean logic deals with the combining of descriptive (subject) terms in special ways.

What do I mean? Earlier we looked at the curious fact that subjects often arrange themselves in pairs, e.g. "Christ and the law"; "Abortion as an ethical issue"; "Freud's view of the unconscious." When we search printed subject indexes, we must search under two or more headings in turn (e.g., under both "Abortion" and "Ethics") because it is not at all easy to combine subject pairs in print.

This can lead to problems. If you are looking at "Abortion as an ethical issue," you can look up "Ethics," but you will find citations to articles on all sorts of ethical issues. You can look up "Abortion," but you will find, besides the articles on the ethical issues, items discussing legal, medical, and social issues.

What you want is a way to link "Abortion" and "Ethics" so that you can pull out only the articles that deal with abortion as an ethical issue. You can't do that well in a printed index. But the task is a relatively simple one for a computer.

Here is where Boolean Logic comes in. For most databases, the searching programs are set up to spot any key term in any title listed in the database. If you ask for "Abortion," the computer will pull out bibliographical information for every article with "Abortion" in its title (including, alas, the occasional deceptive title such as "Secularism as a Sort of Spiritual Abortion").

But if a computer can spot one term in a title, it should also have the capability of spotting more than one term in a title at the same time. What if I ask the computer to pull out only those articles which have the word "Abortion" *and* the word "Ethics" in them? "Secularism as a Sort of Spiritual Abortion" would disappear, and I would get such intriguing titles as "Ethics in the Abortion Issue," and "Modern Abortion: A Dilemma for Christian Ethics." (Plus, perhaps, "The Ethics of Bombing Abortion Clinics." You can't win all the time.)

The goal of Boolean Logic (ways of arranging terms), then, is to focus your search, taking key terms related to your topic and combining them in order to pull out data that could only be found by looking up two or more subject headings in a printed index. Beyond the example just cited, you can use the Boolean common "OR" as in "abortion OR ethics" to get all the articles which have either "abortion" or "ethics" somewhere in their titles. In this case, you are sure to get more items than you would for the "and" command (which demands that both "abortion" and "ethics" appear in every title found), but you will find proportionately more items which are not relevant to your topic.

Other combinations are possible. Suppose you want articles on abortion which do not deal with the ethical issue (but with other issues). You can command, "Abortion NOT ethics." This will net all titles which have "Abortion" but do not have "Ethics" in their wordings.

Multiple combinations can also be made. For example, "Abortion AND ethics OR legal" could find you all the articles where "abortion" and "ethics" appear in the title, plus all the articles whose titles include the words "Abortion" and "Legal." But watch it with multiple commands. Different databases use different rules. The same example on another database could net you all the articles with the key words "Abortion" and "Ethics" plus all the articles with "Legal" in their titles.

You could go further and command, "Abortion AND ethics AND legal," to get only those articles which have all three words in the title. A further caution here: You may be getting too narrow and missing other relevant works because you are demanding too tight a combination of key terms.

One problem with database searching is that titles are not always reliable clues to subject matter. Where a title is obscure, the database may add other key words as enhancements. Even then, it is possible to miss key article citations because the title used a synonym of the word for which you were searching. Computers are incredibly stupid and cannot spot synonyms.

Up to this point, computer databases of bibliographical information have existed far away and have had to be accessed by a modem and a telephone line connection from your computer. This is costly, and many smaller libraries have not been able to afford the equipment and communication costs involved. Even when the equipment was available, such searches were generally conducted only after all other avenues of searching the topic (e.g., printed indexes and bibliographies) were exhausted (and so were the poor students).

Things are changing now mainly due to the compact disk. This amazing little package allows for storage of large amounts of information. Just as exciting is the fact that the equipment to run it is much less prone to breakdowns than are more conventional memory storage systems.

A number of databases are now looking at the possibility of loading much of their information on compact disks and selling them to libraries who can use them on site. *Dissertation Abstracts* is already doing this, as is *Religion Index One and Two, Psychological Abstracts*, ERIC, and so on.

Eventually (dare we dream?) sophisticated computer searching of periodical indexes may be a normal library operation and the printed index virtually a thing of the past. With regular updates available, computer indexes on compact disk could be cheap, current, and profoundly searchable.

Online Library Catalogs

First there was the book catalog (none of us remember that one). Then there were those drawers and drawers of cards. Then came microfiche catalogs. And now—the computer catalog.

More and more libraries today are in the process of replacing their card or microfiche catalogs with a computer terminal. Of course, there are voices raised in protest. "At least," they say, "when I use the card catalog I can know when I've found everything on my subject. Now I have to probe into the void of computer innards and beg for entries to appear on the screen? What if I ask the wrong question? What if the computer is in a bad mood and only gives me half the entries? What if it blows up in my face or says something rude to me? Or (the ultimate question), what if it makes me look like a fool?"

On the other hand there are those who say, "Unless the computer should tell me, I will not believe it." For these people, anything that appears on the screen is sacred and right and complete, for it has come from the god-like inner world of the Machine.

Both views are off-center. The fact is that a computer catalog contains the same sorts of entries as you would find in a card catalog. The advantage is greater search capability. The disadvantage is that no entry is better than the person who put it into the database ("garbage in, garbage out"). Thus there could indeed be flaws, but hopefully few of them.

Let's look at search capability. Remember when we were mining gold from catalog cards and I somewhat sheepishly suggested that you could look up a key subject word in the title catalog, hoping that there was a relevant title beginning with that word? Librarians frown on that and call it an ignorant method.

With computers it isn't ignorant at all. The problem with looking for a key word in a normal title catalog is that you will only succeed if the title begins with that word. But with a computer search, you can use a key word command to pull out all titles containing that word, even if it is the fourth or fifth element in the title. Thus, looking for the title key word "Erasmus," you would find not only *Erasmus and the Growth of Humanism*, but *Studies in the Echiridion of Erasmus*.

Beyond this, depending on how sophisticated the programming is for your computer catalog, you could do Boolean searches, simple subject heading searches, searches isolating books published within a certain range of years on a certain topic, and so on, beyond basic author and title information searching.

All of this, of course, could revolutionize the way we do research—if these catalogs are set up properly. Here is the problem: The more sophisticated the search capability, the less user-friendly the system usually is. Thus some libraries, in order to have a catalog searchable by the uninitiated, have had to sacrifice more complex search methods. The best systems allow users to switch between simple and complex search methods.

Ultimately, then, we are probably looking at a coming golden age for research in which the catalog can become a friend and aid rather than a somewhat treacherous tool.

Full Text

The compact disk promises great things for the future. While I stated earlier that no library will want to put all of its holdings on disks, there are signs that some types of works may be particularly amenable to the compact disks. This is especially true of standard reference sources in which we look for concise information.

An early candidate for disk format was the Grolier Company's *Academic American Encyclopedia*. Encyclopedias are very suitable for computer searching functions since they provide the sort of information which can be easily labeled with suitable headings. Now, not only can you find information on a subject under that subject's main heading, but you can pull out every reference to that subject in any other article.

If I want to find out about the medieval thinker Anselm, I can find not only what the encyclopedia says under "Anslem," but also what it says about Anslem under such article titles as "Scholasticism," "Middle Ages," and "Catholic Church." Such full-text searching could prove useful, especially as more of these works become available on disk.

You are, no doubt, becoming increasingly reconciled to the fact that computers are the new tomorrow. More and more you will find that libraries are becoming havens for terminals and hackers. The benefits will probably be enormous.

7

Case Studies in Successful Research

I have, in the last four chapters, suggested a method for approaching a library to tap from those elusive former trees (books) the rich sap of information you really want. Let's make sure we know the steps in proper order. (I know you hate reviewing, but try to focus anyway. You don't want to carry this manual with you every time you need to do some research.)

- Reference sources. Get a handle on your topic and look for initial information and bibliography in reference articles.

- Preliminary outline. Start one as soon as possible and build on it as you go.

- The catalog. Discover your subject heading(s). Find relevant entries. Mine gold from some of these entries.

- Search of bibliographies in books. Locate a bibliography in a recent book. Find some of the books listed in that bibliography and search through their bibliographies. Locate some of these items and look at their bibliographies, and so on.

- Search for articles in edited books. Scour through *Essay and General Literature Index* or, for a paper on a religion topic, *Religion Index Two*.

- Search for specialized subject bibliographies. Remember that there may or may not be one for your topic.

■ Search the periodical literature. Identify the relevant index(es) and follow the procedure for locating periodical articles.

Now that we have our step in focus, it may be helpful to go through a few actual research projects, following the procedure above.

"The Teenage Suicide Crisis"

My library, for this case, is a theological one of 30,000 volumes, with limited secular material. Thus my search abilities will be somewhat restricted (sound familiar?). I have been given the fascinating topic "The Teenage Suicide Crisis." This must be one of those hot new issues intended to excite and baffle me at the same time.

I begin by manhandling the topic; it looks a bit broad to me. I could look at statistics, discuss how counselors are handling the problem, ask why teenagers attempt suicide, look at the problems of society which lead to a death wish, and so on. Trying to focus the topic, I decide to attempt something like "Recognizing the Signs of the Suicidal Teenager." A "neck-twist" is involved: I want to stress suicide prevention. Having had this approved by a merciful professor, I am ready to begin.

■ Reference Sources. It seems to me that I want to deal with the thoughts and behaviors of suicidal teens. Thought and behavior relate to psychology, so I choose *Baker's Dictionary of Psychology*, looking up the heading "Suicide." While the article I find does not relate particularly to teenagers, it provides a lot of good general information on suicide and gives me a bibliography.

■ Preliminary Outline. I want to focus primarily on signs of suicidal tendency. It might be good to start with a fictional case study to interest the reader and pull the topic out of the abstract. (It might be something like: "George Smith, an active sixteen-year-old, killed himself last week. His friends noticed that he had been acting strangely . . . ."). Then I could analyze common signs and end by discussing options for reacting to the signs and preventing the suicide (dreading, of course, my coming realization that such signs vary and are often unreliable). Thus my outline would be:

I. Case study introduction

II. The signs

III. Prevention

■ The Library Catalog. I discover that "Suicide" is probably my best subject approach. Looking at the subject tracings in the entries I find in the subject catalog, I also discover that "Self-Destructive Behavior" may be helpful. I find several books dealing with suicide in general. Though one series—*Christian Care Books*—discovered on an entry looks helpful, I find that the other volumes in the series are not related to the topic.

I also try the headings "Adolescence" and "Adolescent Psychology," taking note of several books dealing with the problems of teenagers. They will each probably have a section on suicide.

■ Search of bibliographies in books. I will start with:

Marion Duckworth, *Why Teens are Killing Themselves* (San Bernardino: Here's Life, 1987).

Its bibliography yields:

H. Norman Wright, *Crisis Counseling* (1985);
Mary Griffin and Carol Elsenthal, *A Cry for Help* (1981);
Francine Kagsburn, *Too Young to Die* (1976).

Wright's book is interesting; I had not thought of looking at materials on crisis counseling. Kagsburn's book looks like just the sort of thing I need. I locate these books and look at their bibliographies. For example, Wright's book, at the end of his chapter on suicide, lists a book on counseling teenagers and an article on student suicide.

From here, I locate these items and look at their bibliographies, and so on.

- Search for articles in edited books. Looking up "Suicide" in *Religion Index Two (Essay and General Literature Index* is unavailable), I find little beyond a few general articles. Oh well, no one said every strategy would work every time. Let me move on, since this avenue is fruitless.

- Subject bibliographies. I cannot find a specific bibliography on suicide, so I try to find more general works on social problems, adolescence, etc. Again this proves rather fruitless, but I refuse to lose heart.

- Periodical Literature. If this is a hot new issue, periodical literature should be of great help. I decide to look up "Suicide," since "Adolescence" will probably have too many entries to handle easily.

Wow! (Say it softly, this *is* a library). My search paid off. Here are just a few article titles that I found listed in *Religion Index One* (this library does not have *Psychological Abstracts* or *Sociological Abstracts*):

"Churches Respond to Teen Suicide."

"Help Your Teen Avoid Suicide."

"Teen Suicide: A Cry for Help Heard too Late."

"Deadly Cry for Help (Suicide Among the Young)."

"Our Kingdom of Death and Teen Suicides."

The *Christian Periodical Index* guides me from "Suicide" to "Young Adult—Suicidal Behavior," where I find an article entitled:

"At All Cost."

An earlier volume of the same index has, under "Suicide":

"Adolescent Suicide."

The *Guide to Social Science and Religion in Periodical Literature*, once again hard to use, has this article listed under "Social Science" subsection "Youth":

"Half in Love with Easeful Death."

Not bad. For this kind of topic, it looks as if periodical literature is the place where I will find the most current responses to the problem.

"A Significant Figure of the Renaissance Period"

I have been asked, in a course on Renaissance history, to write a paper on a significant figure of the Renaissance period. For some strange reason, I think of Lucrezia Borgia, the sinister femme fatale of the early 1500s.

Though I need basic information, I find that the library I am using is weak in history reference sources. Rather than tossing poor Lucrezia away, I do some lateral thinking. What about general encyclopedias? Rushing to the *Encyclopedia Americana*, I discover the following information:

Lucrezia Borgia (1480–1519), younger sister of Cesare Borgia, was Duchess of Ferrara in Italy. In her lifetime, she married three Italian princes and received a reputation for being corrupt and treacherous. During her later life, she became a patron of the arts and was known for her exemplary behavior. More recent scholarship suggests that her reputation for treachery was not fully deserved—she lived under the influence of her evil father and brother.

The *Americana* also lists a key biography item:

Maria Bellonci, *Lucrezia Borgia* (1953).

I decide to narrow and "neck-twist" my topic into a question: "Who was the real Lucrezia Borgia?"

On to the catalog. Under the subject heading, "Borgia, Lucrezia, 1480–1519," I find only one book:

F. A. Gregorovius, *Lucrezia Borgia, According to Original Documents and Correspondence of her Day* (1960; reprint of 1903).

This looks like just what I need, but it's checked out (sound familiar?).

The time has come for some more lateral thinking. One book (which isn't there) is a pretty poor beginning. And so I ponder the situation. Lucrezia had a brother Cesare. Perhaps there is more information on her brother and perhaps books on Cesare will have information on his sister. I look up "Borgia, Cesare, 1476?–1507," and find:

Bradford, Sarah, *Cesare Borgia: His Life and Times* (1976).

Chamberlin, E. R. *Cesare Borgia* (1969).

Both books have extensive material on Lucrezia. This is good, but I still don't have enough.

Making another lateral, I look up "Italy–History–1268–1492," and discover:

Fusero, Clemente, *The Borgias* (1966).

The heading "Italy–History–1492–1559" gives me:

Brucker, Gene A. *Renaissance Italy: Was it the Birthplace of the Modern World?* (1958).

The heading "Renaissance–Italy" yields:

Burkhardt, Jakob Christoph, *The Civilization of the Renaissance in Italy* (1937).

Chambers, D. S. *Patrons and Artists in the Italian Renaissance* (1970). (Lucrezia was a patron of the arts, remember?)

I decide to try a book bibliography search, since my materials are still rather weak for a major paper. Locating Sarah Bradford's *Cesare Borgia,* I come up with the following:

Bellonci, M., *Lucrezia Borgia* (1953). (This is the item listed after the *Americana* article.)

Gregorovius, F., *Lucrezia Borgia* (1903) (I already located this through the catalog, but it is unavailable).

Mallett, M., *The Borgias: The Rise and Fall of a Renaissance Dynasty* (1969).

Rolfe, F. W., *Chronicles of the House of Borgia* (1901).

Whilfield, J. H., "New Views Upon the Borgias" *History* 27 (1943) (a periodical article).

At this point, I could locate some of these items and search their bibliographies.

It's time to search for articles in edited books and specialized bibliographies. I do that and achieve the following results:

From the *Essay and General Literature Index:*

Lehrman, L. "Renaissance Profiles" in *Vogue's First Reader*, p. 397–402.

From the *Bibliography Index:*

Erlanger, Rachel, *Lucrezia Borgia: A Biography* '78 p347–55 annot (which tells me that this book has an annotated bibliography).

Moving on to periodical indexes, I discover to my horror that the library I am working in does not have *Historical Abstracts*. Refusing to admit defeat, I go to a more general source—*Humanities Index*—and find:

Prizer, W. F., "Isabella d'Este and Lucrezia Borgia as Patrons of Music" *J Am Musicol Soc* 38:1–33 Spr. '85.

That's all it lists. I need more periodical literature! Lateral thinking leads me to the realization that *Biography Index* might be relevant since Lucrezia, despite the accusations of some, was undoubtedly a person. This index lists both books and articles. I find the following:

Chamberlin, E. R., *Fall of the House of Borgia* (1974).

Erlanger, Rachel, *Lucrezia Borgia: A Biography* (1978).

Janeway, E. "Femmes Fatales" *N Y Times Mag* p. 25 Ap. 18 '54.

Suida, W. E. "Lucrezia Borgia in Memorium" *Gaz Geaux-Arts* 35:275–84, 307–8 Ap. '49.

While I may have to go to other libraries to get some of these materials, I now have a good list to work with.

"Behaviorism"

It's psychology term paper time, and I've chosen the topic "Behaviorism." Not feeling inclined to write on methods of training lab rats, I decide to focus on the work of a key figure in this school of psychology. But who?

The Encyclopedia of Psychology, edited by Corsini, under the heading "Behaviorism," reveals that B. F. Skinner was a prominent radical behavorist who argued that whatever cannot be observed in the study of people does not exist. We do not work with internal factors such as mind and myth, but only with the observable.

The same reference source, under Skinner's name, tells me that he wrote a novel of sorts called *Walden Two*, in which he described a Utopia based on the proper application of behavioristic principles. Since I have been looking for some light reading anyway, I sign the book out and have a closer look at it. While a bit boring (there are no villains), *Walden Two* reveals a strange and, to me, frightening world where human freedom does not exist but everyone seems happy anyway.

A theme emerges. I will look at Skinner's behaviorism through a study of *Walden Two*, focusing in my conclusions on Skinner's lack of appreciation of the roles of human depravity and the power of our natural desire for freedom, factors I have already perceived in my initial reading of the book.

I see very early that I will have to watch my biases. It is going to be very important that I understand Skinner correctly and describe his views properly. Thus I move to the catalog to get a list of books Skinner himself has written. I find eight of them listed, two of which seem to be of particular importance: *Beyond Freedom and Dignity* (1971), and *Upon Further Reflection* (1987! Since *Walden Two* was published in 1948, perhaps this book will reveal a shift in views).

The catalog also provides great help when I look up Skinner as a subject (remember, names can act as subjects). Relevant titles include the following:

B. F. Skinner, Consensus and Controversy (1986).

The Skinner Primer (1974).

B. F. Skinner's Behaviorism (1982).

Beyond the Punitive Society (1973—could this one be related to *Walden Two*?).

There are several more, and I realize that I probably will have enough book literature without an extensive book bibliography search, though I will continue to look at bibliographies and footnotes of whatever books I use.

So far I have materials by and about Skinner. Most of the latter should have information on the message of *Walden Two*, but I am now hoping to find items which focus more on Skinner's view of a Utopian society.

I could check *Essay and General Literature Index* and *Bibliographic Index*, but I am running late and so decide to get directly into periodical literature. Choosing *Psychological Abstracts,* I look up Skinner (since *Walden Two* is not really a valid subject heading). By the time I have gone back to 1978 and found nothing (!) on his views in *Walden Two,* I am wondering if I am using the right source.

Time for some lateral thinking. *Walden Two* describes the proposed application of psychological principles to a social situation. Perhaps I should back up a bit and choose a source like *Social Sciences Index,* which covers both psychology and sociology (as well as political science).

Pay dirt! I find articles like:

"Criticism and Response in the Skinner Controversies."

"Skinner's Dark Year and *Walden Two*" (with a bibliography).

"Skinner on the Word Good: A Naturalistic Semantic for Ethics."

"Limits of Behaviorism: A Review Essay on B. F. Skinner's Social and Political Thought."

"Pigeons, People and Paradise: Skinnerian Technology and the Coming of the Welfare Society."

It occurs to me that book reviews of *Walden Two* could be important. In *Book Review Digest* (1948), there are a number of review excerpts. *Book Review Index* reveals the existence of reviews right up into the 1980s.

I now have sufficient information to write a strong analytical paper.

PART III
Doing Battle

8

The Connoisseur Reader, or the Art of Selective Studying

It is all very well to amass an enormous bibliography and have all of your sources scattered artfully on your desk. But if you are assuming that your essay is now as good as written, you are either terribly naïve (which I cannot believe of you) or you plan to copy whole passages verbatim from your sources and pass this off as your essay (which is unthinkable for someone of your sterling character).

Having dismissed both possibilities, I must assume that you realize that getting the materials is only half the battle. Now you have to read them. This chapter, therefore, majors on the arts of reading and note taking. The next chapter will tell you how to organize your notes.

Reading for the Connoisseur and the Glutton

With a tantalizing heading like that, you may want to head for the nearest cafeteria. But read on—food for the mind is better than french fries.

Our generation is very big on what is commonly called "escapist fiction." This is the kind of book that makes no claim to be great literature with deep themes but does promise to take you out of yourself and into a far more exciting world.

I, like many librarians, enjoy reading—adventure stories, spy novels, and such. This does get me dubious glances when I talk about it in some circles, but I am amazed at how many theology professors and even respectable pastors read the same stuff.

DOING BATTLE

The advantage of a thriller is that it lets you escape. You can lie back and let it happen without pondering or analyzing too deeply. You just have to let the skilled thriller writer feed you the adventure until you scream for mercy. Escapist fiction is for gluttons.

I do not, however, label a well-crafted murder mystery novel as escapist in the same sense. The writer of this kind of work dares you at every point to find out not only who did it, but how whoever did it did it. In other words, such a writer does not want you to swallow the novel whole (as in the thriller) but to read it with discernment, picking at each clue with reserve and intelligence. The well-crafted mystery novel is for connoiseeurs.

Where is all this leading? Simply to this basic statement: *research is not for gluttons.*

Consider the problem you face: You have twenty-five scattered sources waiting to be read. They comprise 3,423 pages in total. At an average rate of one page every two minutes, this will take you 6,846 minutes to read, or, in more familiar terms, 114.1 hours. If you skip classes for two weeks and read 8.15 hours per day, you will have it all read. But wait a minute (even though you have none of those to spare)—I haven't allowed the time you need to take notes on what you're reading. You'd better allow three weeks.

Before I take you too far into the realm of the ridiculous, I think you can see that there is no way you will be able to read and take notes on 3,423 pages for one essay. The approach which works so well for devouring spy novels—gluttony—is going to sink you when you research a paper. There has to be a way to pick and choose the best parts.

Let me show you the the connoisseur's approach to reading:

Be Ruthless

You may not like what I have to say now, but I have to say it. Any book you read for research purposes must be used and discarded as quickly as possible. Forget that the author probably worked long into the night to produce the book, while his neglected wife and children waited, weeping, at his study door. Forget that he had such a deep sense of mission that it consumed him twenty-four hours a day until he could put it into print.

You need information. The book you are reading has information. Your problem is that it has too much information or that some of the information is not relevant to your essay topic. Thus you must use every skill you can muster to get the information you need without dallying to read the rest.

At this point I must warn you—do not show this chapter to any professor. He or she might burn the whole book right in front of you. Professors are purists, and rightly so. They have written one or more theses for which they actually did read all 3,423 pages, plus 783,459 more. They got into the heart and soul of the authors they were reading and they learned to like it.

You, on the other hand, are writing a term paper that is due, along with two others, in nine days. Be ruthless. Read what you need and abandon the rest. It's your only hope.

One big note of caution: Be sure that you read enough to understand what the writer is saying. It is all very good to be efficient and discerning (the connoisseur) rather than a sponge (the glutton), but be very sure you have grasped not only what the author is saying but why the author is saying it.

More on this soon.

Get to Know the Material Without Reading It All

No, this is not a call to do skimpy research. This is an attempt to show you how to zero in on what you need without missing anything important.

Here are the steps, first for books and then for articles:

Books

First, have a good look at the title page, preface, foreword, and introduction. A book is not just a series of paragraphs. There is a motive, a plan, and the preliminary pages can often give you solid clues as to what these may be.

Title pages are often ignored because they seem to have so little information. But they can be important. Be sure to look at both the title and the subtitle of the book. Increasingly I am finding that the title is just there to be cute, while the subtitle explains what the book is about. Consider these gems:

> *Ante Pacem: Archaeological Evidences of Church Life before Constantine.*
>
> *Lifestyle: Conversations with Members of the Unification Church.*
>
> *Passages: Predictable Crises of Adult Life.*

DOING BATTLE

The preface, foreword, or introduction will often tell you what the author is attempting to do in the book. There you can look for a basic theme, as well as for a description of the approach to the subject and of the material to be covered. Reading a good preface can sometimes give you all the clues you need to get into the really important data.

Second, check out the table of contents. This forms the skeleton upon which the body is hung, the keystone that supports the building, the street signs which give meaning to the metropolis, the—

But why go on? The point is simply that the table of contents provides you with the basic structure of the book in its proper order. Here we can get into the good, the bad, and the useless. There was a time when tables of contents provided main headings, subdivisions, and even short paragraph summaries of the main arguments. Now chances are that all of the chapter headings will be cute but uninformative. Still, it is worth your while to check the table of contents. It may help you zero in on the chapter you really want. And it gives you a sense of the writer's whole development of the topic.

Third, have a look at the index. Indexes can be good, atrocious, or nonexistent. Their real value (when present) lies in their ability to locate specific information when the book itself covers a broader topic. In religious books, indexing has sometimes outdone itself. You can find Scripture indexes, Greek and Hebrew word indexes, indexes to ancient authors, indexes to modern authors, as well as the traditional subject index.

Balancing the indexing against the information in the table of contents can help you greatly by taking you right to the good stuff in the book. It can, but beware of two problems.

- Indexes often list many page numbers after each subject heading, forcing you to do a lot of looking up to find what you want. Comparing chapter headings with page numbers in the index might help you speed up the process by locating the most relevant sections.

- When you have located a subject through an index, watch out for the natural tendency to take information out of context. Remember that the paragraph you are reading on page 294 was preceded by 293 pages of argumentation.

Fourth, give the book a run-through, even if you are only using a part of it. The run-through includes:

- Reading opening and concluding portions of each chapter to see what the author intended to cover and what he or she concluded.

- Looking up subheadings in the body of each chapter.

- Checking to see if the author has a chapter at the end of the book stating a summary or conclusion.

- Possibly looking up a book review or two if the book is confusing or potentially controversial.

Fifth, when it comes to reading the appropriate portion(s) of the book, be a connoisseur of the argumentation, not a glutton who does not care what he is eating as long as he is eating. Ask yourself, What is the author saying? Where is he or she coming from in this? (background and motivation). Is the author really dealing with the issues? How? How does his or her treatment compare or contrast with those of other people you are reading? What has been avoided or inadequately covered?

And so on. Don't merely absorb (gluttony). Analyze. Get involved. It will help your paper immeasurably.

Articles

With a periodical article you lack some of the more familiar signposts—tables of contents, indexes, sometimes even sub-headings in the text. To add to the problem, the writer may argue a complex point over several pages without stating a conclusion until the end. How do you get at the article's message in short order and make good use of it?

First, find an abstract if you can locate one quickly. The most generous periodicals actually provide their own abstracts in the text of their publications. If this is not the case for your article, it may well be abstracted in one of the tools we described in chapter 5. With a good abstract, you can at least discern the author's main points and conclusions.

Second, watch for key propositions. There are patterns to expository writing. Some authors state a position and then spend a paragraph or ten supporting it. Others take a great deal of space to marshall the evidence before they come up with a conclusion. In either case, what you are looking for is a sentence or two in which the author tells you what he or she really thinks. When you have found it, you can distinguish it from the author's argumentation.

Third, check out the author's main conclusions. Some authors are very frustrating here. They spend pages arguing something and then come up with some inane statement like, "The conclusion is obvious" (but not to their readers) or, "This evidence demonstrates our point" (but you can't, for the life of you, find where they stated their point in the first place).

Simply grin and bear it. Assume that the writer will state some conclusions and be grateful when they are there.

Fourth, if you can find no clues to guide you, read the whole article. There are times when you will just have to muddle through. But it won't hurt you too much. As you go, try to abstract the article yourself on paper. If you ever have to refer to it again (in a week when you've forgotten that you read it), you want to be one step ahead of your first attempt.

Conclusions

We are talking about the hard realities here—too little time and too much to read. Perhaps one day professors will allow students to do larger projects that cross course boundaries. But until that time, you need to know how to practice discriminating reading.

Remember that books are sources of information. Develop those skills which will help you to extract that information with the greatest speed and efficiency. But beware of quoting a writer out of context because you did not read enough of the context. More on this shortly.

Note Taking

Trying to teach someone to take notes is almost like trying to teach a baby sparrow to fly. Most of what it takes comes from within you, not from my instructions. I can flap my arms and show you the motions, but you have to develop the will and skill to soar above the clouds.

One of the biggest problems most students face is that they take too many notes that will later go unused. The key to this problem is to formulate and use a preliminary outline as soon as possible in the research process. If you are one of those people who prepares the outline while your typist is rattling off page 15 of your completed paper, you have probably wasted a

90

lot of time taking notes that ended up in the round file beside your desk.

Once you have a clear vision of what you want to learn and cover in the paper, you must next decide on a note-taking style:

The Determined Photo-copier

For some students, note-taking is easy. Armed with fourteen dollars in dimes, they simply photocopy everything that looks important, take all 140 copies home, and assemble an essay. Would that most of us could afford this method.

A bit of advice here:

☞ If you are using the copier, make sure that you write down the author, title, place of publication, publisher, and date on every sheet you copy. You would be surprised at how many people later wander the library, wayward photocopy in hand, looking desperately for whatever book they took it from.

☞ Use a highlight pen on your copies as soon as you have made them, while the information you have been reading is still fresh in your mind. You want to mark the passages which were of greatest importance to you so that you will not, sometime later, have to read all of each copied page.

☞ Remember that you are at a disadvantage if you copy. "Me?" you smirk. "I'm the one with fourteen dollars in dimes. I'll have everything done in one-tenth the time it takes these long-hand scribblers around here." Yes, but recognize that you have probably interacted with your material at a far more superficial level than have those "longhand scribblers." When you go home tonight and try to wade through all 140 copies, you may find that you have entered a strange and cruel world in which no landmarks make sense to you and the reasons why you made at least half of the copies totally escape you.

☞ If you want to copy, make sure that you read thoroughly (don't you hate the word "thoroughly?") what you've copied either in its original state just before you push the copy button or in its duplicated state the same day you make the copy. If you do the latter, you may even find out in time that you copied the wrong page.

The Quoter

Some people like to copy direct quotations from books or articles. There are some distinct advantages and disadvantages:

Advantages

- You will not have to go back to the book later on if you need a suitable quotation. It will be right in your notes.

- A quote can give you greater accuracy. This is particularly important if the subject is still rather new to you. Even when you do not fully understand a writer's argument, you can copy a paragraph that states it. Later on, when you are more in tune with the subject, the quote may make more sense to you. Since you copied it directly, you do not have to question its accuracy (unless you copied it wrongly).

- The mere act of copying helps you to get to know the material more intimately, since copying demands that you read the material slowly and, in fact, that you read each word several times. In understanding, you will be far ahead of the photocopier when your notes are complete.

Disadvantages

- The process can become long and laborious.
- You must be very careful to quote enough to catch the context. Alternatively, you could summarize the context in your notes and then copy directly the portion which is most important to you.

The Summarizer

This person reads a chunk of material and then summarizes it in his or her own words. The point is to condense several pages of what you are reading into a paragraph of notes or a paragraph into a sentence.

92

Advantages

- This method is quicker than quoting.

- The process of summarizing forces you to think about the material and make it your own.

Disadvantages

- The method does not work well if you are dealing with difficult material whose complexity makes it hard to condense.

- You will have to go back to the book if you find that you later want a quotation.

- You have to be very careful that you understand correctly the things you are reading. If you misinterpret, you have no way of checking for accuracy later, other than going back to your source material.

The Paraphraser

The difference between summarizing and paraphrasing is that the former condenses material while the latter rewrites each sentence in the reader's own words. With a paraphrase, you can expect that your paragraph of notes will be as long as the book's paragraph, if not longer.

Advantage

- This method is great if your material is very complex and only sentence by sentence unraveling will make sense of it.

Disadvantages

- This method takes you longer than quoting, because you have to think through each sentence you write.

- Your notes will be as long as your source material.

- There is a constant risk of misinterpretation of your source.

Which Method is Best?

I suggest that you could use all of these methods, applying each one to the type of material for which it is best suited:

☞ If what you are reading is long but vitally important or if your material has charts, graphs, etc. of importance, you may want to photocopy.

☞ If you can find reasonably short sections which summarize the author's view in a concise and striking way, you may want to do a brief note on the context and then quote directly.

☞ If your material is not overly detailed and you want only an overview of what the writer is saying, then summarize.

☞ Only if your material is almost incomprehensible is paraphrasing a useful method. I would suggest photocopying the original so that you can later compare the original with your paraphrase.

Further Points on Note Taking

☞ If you are quoting, use quotation marks in your notes. If the material you are reading turns a page but the quote continues, put a slash mark or some other indication in your notes to tell you where the page has turned in the original. *Always* indicate, at the bottom of the quote, the number(s) of the page(s) on which the quotation appeared.

☞ If you are summarizing, conscientiously work at using your own wording. If you find that your wording is turning out like a clone of the original, then quote directly or photocopy. With summaries, indicate in the margin of your notes the book pages you are summarizing (in case you want to go back to the book later).

☞ If an insight comes to you as you are reading, include it in your notes. Put square brackets around it and end the statement of your insight with a dash and your initials. This will tell you for sure that this is your material. What do I mean by an insight? I mean reaction positively or negatively to what you are reading, a discovery that your author compares or contrasts well with something else you've been reading, or a creative thought which might add to the argument.

☞ Make sure you leave nothing out of your notes: full information on author, title, place, publisher, date, page numbers, etc. You don't want to have to relocate a book you've already read. Chances are that someone else will have taken it out by then, and you will never find out what page that key quotation came from.

A Gentle Warning About a Horrible Crime

Just to end the chapter on a cheery note, let me caution you about the academic crime of *plagiarism*. Plagiarism, to put it simply, is passing off someone else's work as your own. The following examples, if they describe your actions, place you very obviously among the guilty. You are plagiarizing if you:

- Quote directly from a book or periodical without acknowledging that the material is not yours;

- Paraphrase an author, sentence by sentence, without acknowledging that author;

- Use without acknowledgment an idea put forward by an author when you cannot find the same idea in two or more other independent sources. (The point is that concepts that are unique to an author need to be acknowledged, while more generally used information does not.)

Plagiarism is an academic crime because it is the theft of someone else's creativity, because it is a misrepresentation of your own knowledge and abilities, and because most astute professors catch offenders quite easily and then feel hurt that they have been lied to. This often results in a zero for the paper and, perhaps, further disciplinary action.

9

Organizing Your Notes to Write Your Paper

"I have seventy-five pages of notes, not counting the photocopy I left on the copier and the two pages which I think fell behind my desk. Now every time I look at these collections of chicken scratch, I want to scream. What a mess! How am I ever going to make an essay out of this chaos? Will there ever be meaning to my life?"

Yes, there will. Take heart. There is a way to organize your disastrous jumble, no matter how incomprehensible it now seems to be.

I hesitate whenever I suggest "my method" for note organization. What if your mind, heaven forbid, does not correspond with mine? What if I am totally out of touch with the logical categories you most enjoy?

Still, someone has to suggest something. Librarians, even if dull, are undoubtedly logical and thus better equipped than, say, Renaissance painters, to suggest ways of organizing information. I am giving you only one method (with a variation on it at one point) because throwing too many methods at you can be confusing. If you do not like this approach, speak to your favorite professor and ask for another one.

I call my system the "register method of note organization." A "register" is a listing or running series of bits of information. The way the register itself is organized is not particularly important because you find information in it through an indexing system.

Let's see how this method works in, for example, an automobile parts shop. The parts are laid out in neat rows of bins on the shelves. The fact that the water system thermostats are next to the distributer caps, which are next to the spark plugs, is not nearly as relevant as the fact that each bin has a big number on it.

When I walk in and ask for a thermostat for a 1939 Wuzzly roadster, the parts man does not proceed immediately to the shelves and start looking. He opens a big parts book or searches some microfiche to find the number of the bin that contains my thermostat. Armed with that number, he can retrieve the part easily.

Here is the point of the analogy: The rows of auto parts are your jumbled mess of notes. The bin numbers are codes you insert into these notes. The parts book represents the indexing of your notes. This is how it works.

Your Notes

Some people write notes on 3 x 5 or 4 x 6 cards. This is, in my humble opinion, a grave error. Even an average-sized article requires two or three cards, covered with writing on both sides. A book increases the number of cards required to twenty or thirty. Not only is that costly, but you know you are going to lose at least a few cards between the library and your home or dorm room.

If God had meant us to write out notes on cards, he would not have allowed us to invent standard notepaper. It's as simple as that. Does not nature itself tell you that eyes, hands, and pens were made for writing boldly on decently-sized paper instead of scraping one-sixteenth inch high letters on minuscule cards?

Save your cards for the next part of my system, and write your notes the natural way—on lined, punched, normal notepaper. Be sure, however, to follow the right method. As you begin notes on each book or article, be very certain that you write down full bibliographical information (author, title, place, publisher, date). Then write your notes.

When you have completed your notes for a particular item (even if those notes are ten pages long), simply leave a few lines blank and then start on your next book or article, being sure again to enter full bibliographical information first.

One of the most important things you need to do with your notes is to *number the pages consecutively*. If you have fifty pages of notes on ten books, then number your note pages from one to fifty. If you have photocopies, put them in the right places in

your notes and number them too. Be sure you keep your notes
in a binder so that they won't get jumbled.

Your Author Index

As you move along in your research, you need to begin
preparing an index to your notes. For this purpose, you will
need 3 x 5 or 4 x 6 cards, which are, admittedly, easy to lose.
May I suggest that you keep them in a small file box or at least
secure them with a rubber band?

What do you include on such cards? Each one will indicate
one of the sources (book, periodical article, etc.) you are using
for your paper:

☞ At the top of the card write full bibliographical
information (author, title, place, publisher, date,
etc.) according to the format demanded by your
school (see the *Appendix* for illustrations of format). This entry should be written as it would
appear in the bibliography of your paper.

☞ Below this, write the page number(s) of your
notes for this particular item and circle the
number(s). For example, if you have taken notes
of F. F. Bruce, *Israel and the Nations*, the card will
have at the top full bibliographical information.
Below this, you will show that pages 4–10 of your
notes cover this book. (This is why you need to
number every page of your notes.)

☞ As your file grows, you can arrange it in alphabetical order by author. Thus this card file will
become, in effect, your bibliography in proper
sequence. As well, it will tell you where your
notes are for each item you have read.

A colleague who has quarrelled with my method suggests
that the cards could be eliminated if you arranged your notes in
alphabetical order by author of the book or article. Using a ring
binder, this would not be too much of a problem. Yet I have
some hesitation at this. Much as I would like to get rid of the
cards, it is not all that easy to find a particular section of notes
even if arranged alphabetically by author. The cards enable
quick access to any item you have read.

Your Subject Index

You need to have some way of getting at the subject matter of your notes. Thus this second index is needed. It can be set up in a number of ways. Let me first detail the normal method for a term paper of up to about twenty pages:

I have been suggesting since early on in this book that it is important to formulate a preliminary outline of your paper as soon as possible in the research process. Now you will see how such an outline can pay off:

☞ Take a good-sized piece of paper and put your preliminary outline on it, leaving as much space between each heading as possible.

☞ Determine a symbol to represent each heading (and subheading if you have any), and write it on your sheet of paper. That symbol now represents that heading. You can use stars, triangles, squares, and so on.

☞ Go through your notes and, with different colored pens, put the symbols from each outline heading opposite the notes that will help you write that section of your paper. For example, if your heading was "An Introduction to Behaviorism" (see my example below), you would put the appropriate symbol for that heading (in my case, the symbol @) opposite any notes that explain about behaviorism in general.

☞ Whenever you put a symbol down in your notes, write the page number for that note under the heading in your outline. Have a look at this example:

The Limits of Behaviorism: *Walden Two* in perspective

  I. An Introduction to Behaviorism.
     @ 4, 17, 32, 43

 II. B. F. Skinner's *Walden Two*.
     + 4, 22, 25–34, 42

III. *Walden Two* as a Demonstration of the Limits of Behaviorism.
     % 16, 18, 23, 36–40, 42

In the above example, my symbols are @, +, and %. The numbers are the pages of my notes that have been marked with the different symbols for each section of the paper. Thus, on page 22 of my notes I will find the + symbol, indicating that this section deals with *Walden Two*.

DOING BATTLE

Why go to all this trouble? To answer, let me describe the awful alternative. You begin writing the actual paper and get to heading number one: "An Introduction to Behaviorism." Now you have to read through all forty-seven pages of notes, looking for material on this aspect. Having found your material and written this section of your paper, you move on to the next heading and repeat the process. Again you read all forty-seven pages of notes, looking for material on your second section. For heading number three, your notes must again be reread.

If you would have read through your notes thoughtfully and in detail, applying symbols from your outline headings and putting appropriate note page numbers on your outline, you would have had to read all of the material only once. A further reading of selected portions would complete the process.

Thus the use of an outline as the skeleton of a subject index to your notes can save you a lot of time in the long run. Besides, it gives you a warm and comforting sense of being organized before you actually started writing. When was the last time you had a feeling like that?

Subject Indexing for Longer Assignments

Once you begin to move into longer papers and theses, the one-page outline subject index becomes a thing only to dream about. Now you may have ten major headings (or chapters) with twelve subheadings each. How will you ever organize a monster like that?

Remember, whatever method you use, to do your subject indexing as you go along. If you want to be guaranteed a "climbing Mount Everest in bare feet" experience, do all your note taking for a thesis and then try to subject index 1,400 pages of notes in one fell swoop.

One method of subject indexing for larger papers is the subject card index. This is similar to a library's subject catalog, but now you are indexing subjects dealt with in your notes. Perhaps the closest parallel is the index at the back of a book. With this method, each card would have a subject term and then a list of the page numbers of the notes where that subject is treated.

There are some problems with this method. First, it can be hard to come up with a single term for a subject. Second, you have to watch out for inadvertent synonyms. You might find out that you have indexed a single subject under two related headings. Third, you might lose a subject, that is, forget what strange term you used to describe it and later have a great deal of fun trying to locate the material on it in your notes. Fourth, it is sometimes hard to get an alphabetic subject file and a thesis outline working together in harmony.

Perhaps the most practical solution is to do what you would do for a term paper but on a larger scale. For example, you could write your ten-point and 120-subpoint outline on a huge sheet of paper and hang it on your wall like a map. More reasonably, you could use several sheets of standard notepaper, applying one major heading to each sheet so that you have lots of room for subheading and page number listings. The result would be ten sheets of paper, which you could arrange in proper outline order. Alternatively, you could use a file of 3 x 5 cards arranged in the order of your outline. For each main heading, you could tape a tab on the top of the card, and arrange cards for your subheading behind each main heading. The page numbers on each card would tell you where in your notes that heading or subheading is discussed.

Whatever method you use, you want to have a way of keying your note material to your outline so that as you write the paper, you need to read your notes only a minimum number of times. The confidence that comes from knowing that you can find what you need in your notes is something that can improve your whole outlook and probably your grades as well.

A Note on Computers and Note Organization

Anything a human can organize, a computer can organize faster and better. When it comes to producing indexes, no one can beat the little mechanical clerk.

Thus it was inevitable, I suppose, that programs for note organization would come on the market. I don't intend to give you the details for any one brand, but I will try to provide a general idea of some of the things they can do:

- They have the ability to allow you to enter notes in such a way that notes or portions of them can be retrieved by bibliographic citation (author or title) or by key words in the text.

- Some provide a system of "windowing" by which notes from a number of sources may be seen on sections of the screen all at the same time. Thus you may compare and contrast at will.

- They usually provide word processing but include special features for scholars like yourself: formatting of bibliography items according to the format demanded by your school, proper placement of footnotes, and so on.

Some cautions must be raised, however. First, you have to get your notes into the computer. This means (until decent reading machines are available) typing them all in. Second, while the computer is well able to search for key words, it is not smart enough to see additional material related to the subject that does not contain the key words. Thus to be sure that you have everything from your notes that you wanted to include, you will probably have to read through your note database.

Ah, computers. The joy and the pain. Increasingly, I suspect, they will replace the pen as the student's most important tool.

10

Tips on Research Writing

At last we come to the end. I hope that this chapter will help you when you face outlining and writing problems.

The Outline

Outlining is a major problem in research papers. If you are attempting (in fear, no doubt) a thesis, you will probably find that coming up with a good outline is the highest hurdle you will have to leap.

Let's visualize the problem first. The reason why the outline is troublesome is that people receive information in sequence rather than absorbing all of the facts at the same time. Simply because a twenty-page paper may take ten or fifteen minutes to read means that some information must be presented before other information is given.

Let's look at it in another way. An argument (that is, a statement of a case or a proposition) is like a house. You have to lay the foundation before you can move to the upper stories. Everything depends on what has already been laid down. We move from what is known to what is added. Thus a construction sequence is required.

Perhaps the best way to learn how to outline is to look at specific steps and see these illustrated with specific examples.

Step One: The Theme

As we have seen, the first task in putting together even a preliminary outline is figuring out what you want to do with the paper and writing a theme statement in a sentence or two. Let's choose "Burnout in the Workplace Today." Having narrowed and "neck-twisted" it, we come up with this theme:

> By recognizing the stages of burnout and taking appropriate counter-measures, the worker can survive the stresses of the job environment.

Step Two: The Headings

Now you need to analyze your written theme to see which areas or issues are going to need coverage in your paper. *Do not worry about order for the moment*. Simply list the areas as they come to mind. If none occur to you, go back to your reference sources and see how the topic is normally subdivided.

In our example, we can isolate at least two major issues:

- counter-measures against burnout
- stages of burnout

Step Three: Arranging the Headings

This is usually the hardest part. What you want is a logical order. Here are some tips:

☞ Get general and introductory matters out of the way first. In our example, we will probably have to define burnout and show that workers are susceptible to it before we can begin looking at the topic in depth. Perhaps a fictional case history of burnout (Henrietta Sledge, who was deliberately never given a job description so they could work her to death) could form a compelling introduction.

☞ Look for a natural order. In our example, the very fact that we will be looking, in one portion, at the stages of burnout suggests an order: stage one, stage two, and so on.

Let's look at a few other natural order clues:

First, in a historically-oriented paper (e.g. "The Early Conquests of Alexander the Great"), you can move the account along chronologically.

Second, in an analysis of issues, you can follow an ascending order, looking at smaller factors or arguments first and moving on to the really crucial factors. Your last section could begin, "The most serious difficulty with . . . , however, is . . ."

Third, in a paper contrasting or comparing two viewpoints, there are basically two ways of going about it. You can take the longitudinal approach by which you discuss one view in its entirety and then bring in the second view, making appropriate comparisons and contrasts. Or you can do a cross-sectional study. Here you break each view down into its component arguments. You present an argument from one side and the counterargument from the other. Then you return to the first side for a second argument, followed by a further counterargument, and so on. In this way, if contrasting positions are being discussed, you are allowing the opponents to meet toe to toe and punch/counterpunch their way through the whole issue.

☞ Deal with descriptive (objective) issues before you analyze (become subjective). In our example, it is better to lay out the commonly understood and accepted stages of burnout before you make your own suggestions as to how burnout could be nipped in the bud. The stages are part of objective knowledge. Your suggestions for attacking burnout are more likely to be open to debate.

Here I must mount my soap-box for a few moments. When I state that proper outline order is description before analysis, I am also saying that every viewpoint has a right to a fair hearing before you criticize it.

Suppose you are doing a paper on the well known (at least to me, since I created him, so to speak) social scientist Horace Q. Blowhard, who has had the audacity to argue that the death penalty should be instituted for traffic offenses. Your paper, "Why Don't You Stand in Front of *My* Car, Horace?", intends to rip the man to shreds. How will you do this most effectively?

If you are still learning some of the fine points of intellectual maturity, you may want to begin by saying, "Horace Q. Blowhard lives up to his name. If there ever was a reason for tar and feathers, Horace (no friend of yours or mine) would be it." From here, your outline would be:

    I. Condemnation of Blowhard.

    II. Some of the Most Vile of his Views.

    III. Concluding Condemnation.

But this is utterly the wrong approach. O ye contenders for justice and all it stands for, halt and lend your ears. *No one deserves to be torched verbally or in print before he has been understood.* Not even Horace Q. Blowhard.

In a paper analyzing the views of anyone or the issues involved in any controversy, begin with an objective, unbiased, fair statement of the arguments being made, no matter how much you may despise these arguments and/or their proponents.

Devastating attacks do not belong on the first, or even the third, page of paper. They belong in the second half, after a clear statement of the facts as they are known. If you see no need to be courteous to Horace, at least consider your reader. Does not he or she deserve to know what there is to know about Dr. Blowhard's opinions before you turn your reader's heart against the man?

"Describe before you analyze" means "Give the views a chance to be heard without editorial comment before you bash them into the ground with your caustic verbiage and ready wit."

Some Tips on Research Writing

This is not a creative writing manual, but there are some things you can do to give your paper the appearance of mature scholarship rather than adolescent purple prose (which, of course, you have never used).

Introduce Your Paper Properly

In your introduction, you need to state the issue you wish to address. If you are writing an analytical paper, your introduction should present the problem in such a way that it is seen as a real problem, thus creating a sense of involvement in the reader. Be sure you demonstrate that the issue is important. Do not state the obvious—"This issue deserves attention . . ."—but imply it by your presentation.

Use personalized illustrations in your introductions. For example, if you are writing about a great figure of history, begin with an anecdote from that person's life as a sort of demonstration of the theme you want to present.

Many professors want you to state your theme or thesis (the point you want to make) in your introduction. If you do so, try to leave the reader with an sense of anticipation: "How is he or she going to prove this one?"

Always Describe Before You Analyze

You thought I had long since fallen off my soapbox. Don't worry, I won't bring it up again. But do it. Your writing will look more mature.

Avoid Ridicule

When you disagree with a certain writer or viewpoint, you must maintain a level of respect and decorum. Your opponent is not a "moron," "idiot," "stupid," or "useless." (Believe it or not, I have seen all of these terms in student papers.) Such language only reflects badly on you.

Be Logical

By this, I mean that whenever you are traveling along a certain train of thought, make sure your reader is still in the caboose behind you. Don't flit around. Don't jump to another track without warning. Always remember that you are writing for someone who doesn't know where you are going. Lead your reader along gently, step by step. Stay on track.

This is where a clear sense of your theme and outline will be of great help. For each paragraph in your paper, ask yourself:

- Is this paragraph in the right place in this paper (i.e. does it match the heading it is under)?

- Does this paragraph contribute to my theme?

Be Explicit

I don't know how many students there are out there (good solid students) who believe in ESP. They assume that their professors can read their every thought even when it is never expressed. Thus we get a gem that looks something like this:

> "In looking at the issues of Nicea, we must focus on the Arian Debate. The facts are well known and thus we move to the specific role of the famous Athanasius in dealing with . . ."

What is a Nicea? What is an Arian Debate? Who's Athanasius? If you don't make it clear, your professor has no way of determining whether you know what you're talking about either.

DOING BATTLE

Aim for Clear Writing Rather than Erudition

The mark of an educated person is not the length of words and sentences used but the ability to communicate complicated truths in plain language. Be concise. Say what you mean. Avoid like the plague every long word where a shorter word would work as well. Try never to be ambiguous.

Watch Out for Flawed Arguments

This includes:

Misrepresenting Authorities. If you are appealing to someone's work as support for your argument, be very sure that you represent him or her correctly. Do not quote out of context, suppress information that would give a more accurate picture, or anything similar. This sort of dishonesty needs to be left to tabloid newspapers ("Senator Frump Denies that He Beats His Dog," when no one but the tabloid writer ever suggested that he did).

Arguments from Origins. Just because a viewpoint emerged from a dubious source does not necessarily make the viewpoint wrong or right. If a country that exploits the poor invents a wonderful machine to help end famine in the world, is the invention of no value simply because the country it came from is exploitative?

A variation of the origins fallacy is the *ad hominen argument*— attacking the person instead of his ideas. While it might seem legitimate to criticize a writer on family unity who has been divorced seven times, you must look at the written material itself. The concepts may be sound, even though the author does not exemplify them.

Arguments from Insufficient Evidence. I am constantly amazed at the way some students skip over weighty problems without proving their point. They use expressions like, "It is obvious . . ." and, "Such a view is unacceptable today . . . ," when much more effort is needed to convince the reader that it really is obvious or unacceptable. My reaction is to assume one of two things: either the writer has not done enough research to discover that a controversy exists, or he has no real evidence to back up his solution and is trying to bluff his way through.

You must make sure you know which points need proving (by the amount of disagreement in your sources) and then treat them seriously by putting together solid evidence to demonstrate which side of the issue is correct. If there is not sufficient evidence available to make a decision (and if you have searched diligently), admit it. Write something like, "There continues to be considerable debate over this issue, and no consensus appears likely until more evidence is found." (Do not write, "I can't understand this issue and so I haven't made up my mind.")

Read the Better News Magazines

No, I am not kidding. Good writing can be learned in part by reading it. In writing essays that are attempting to convey information, a style that is very useful is the style used in better-quality news reporting. (Not, of course, the type you find in those rags in the supermarket: "Baby with Two Heads Born to Seventy-Five-Year-Old Single Mother.")

Know When to Quote and When not to Quote

You should quote:

- When you want to back up your view with that of a prominent scholar who agrees with you.

- When something someone says is catchy or memorable in its wording. For example, Rudolf Flesch, in *The Art of Readable Writing*, commenting on the stuffy, long, complicated sentences in much current academic literature, wrote, "The cure for this type of sentence elephantiasis is very simple. All you need is to stop being stuffy and talk like a human being . . ."

A witty quote can be gold in your essay.

However, you should not quote:

- When you can say it as well in your own words.

- When the material you want to quote is over a paragraph long (unless it is absolutely crucial in its original wording and is necessary to the central theme of your paper).

- When you already have at least one quote per page in your essay. You do not want to fill your paper with quotes. One every two or three pages is ample. Your reader wants to read your wisdom, not necessarily that of everyone else.

DOING BATTLE

Know Some Basic Rules for Quotations

Always present your own material first and then back it up with your quotation. Never let a quotation present new information. Here the issue is one of authority. Every time you present new material with a quote, you are deferring to the authority of your source. That knocks the wind out of your own authority. Let's put it this way: Whose paper is it? It's yours. Stand on your own two feet and make your own statements. Quotations are for back-up and support.

Never, never, never write a paper that strings together quotations with only a few lines of commentary by yourself. Such papers are doomed, since your professor knows that his ten-year-old son could paste together the same quotations. Essays are assigned so that you can think through information and express thoughtful conclusions. Use quotations sparingly.

If you have a source that quotes yet another source, try to find the original source and quote it directly. Only when you cannot locate the original should you use the secondary source. Then in your footnote you should indicate what you are doing: "Raymond Sludge, *The Red Rose*, 47, as quoted in Horace Roebuck, [etc.]."

Know the Uses of Footnotes or Endnotes and Citations

Their purposes include:

- Citing works you have quoted or clearly borrowed ideas from. Most students realize that quotations need to be footnoted. But you also need to footnote borrowed ideas if these are relatively unique. Here's a rule of thumb: If you use an idea that you can only find in the same form in one or two sources, acknowledge your sources with a footnote. If the material is found in three or more sources and you cannot see that these are borrowing the idea from only one source, don't bother with a footnote.

- Stating further bibliography for the reader who may be interested in pursuing the matter. This procedure, while tedious to you, shows the extent of your research and could earn you appreciation and a better grade.

- Citing sources that agree with your position. This is very useful if you've gone out on a limb. The supporting props of five other scholars who agree with you can be reassuring indeed. Begin this type of footnote with "So too, F. F. Bruce, [citation]," or "This position is also held by . . ."

- Defending a certain position against possible objections. Here you are not sure someone will object to what you are saying, but you see a potential flaw in the argument. It is better for you to point out the problem and respond to it before your professor does. A format for this could begin, "It might be objected that . . . but we assert that . . ." This sort of note shows your professor that you are aware of the possible cons as well as the stated pros. If the objection, however, is often raised in the material you are reading, it may be better to deal with it in the actual text of your paper.

- Dealing with a related side issue that might spoil the flow of the essay itself if it were to appear in the text. This use is rare, but you may want to add to the depth of your paper in this way. Don't overdo it, though.

Watch Your Conclusions

A good conclusion summarizes the main focus of your paper and makes your position clear. Avoid flowery, sentimental, or overly long conclusions. Say what you need to say and end it mercifully.

Give Your Essay a Professional Look

It should be well typed with no typographical errors, good spelling, and so on. Professors tend to assume that a sloppy product is evidence of a sloppy mind.

Research can be exciting, even fun. It can be done well, by anyone no matter what their original ability happens to have been. I trust that I have given you enough to develop your skills to do first class work. The rest is up to you.

Appendix

Two Common Formats for Papers

For the past few years, there has been considerable debate over the best format for citing references in essays and for setting up the essays themselves. The traditional method of footnotes or endnotes with a general bibliography at the end of the paper has been challenged by the parenthetical reference system, which is in vogue in the social sciences. At last report, the parenthetical system is winning the day and may soon become common even in writing for the humanities.

As well, the traditional form of title page for term papers is beginning to give way to an approach which incorporates the title information into the first page of the essay itself. With all this diversity, a good number of professors lay down specific instructions for their students as to what is, and what is not, acceptable.

The two standard sources for information on style are:

> Kate L. Turabian, *A Manual for Writers of Term Papers, Theses, and Dissertations*, 5th ed. (Chicago: University of Chicago Press, 1987).

> Joseph Gibaldi and Walter S. Achtert, *MLA Handbook for Writers of Research Papers*, 3d ed. (New York: Modern Language Association of America, 1988).

Turabian continues to support the traditional footnote and endnote systems for the humanities, as well as the more widely accepted separate title page. MLA has opted for the parenthetical system for all types of papers and supports elimination of a separate title page.

■■■

While there are some variations, the common thread of

APPENDIX

parenthetical reference systems lies in the virtual elimination of footnotes and endnotes (except for extended discussions of issues) in favor of brief citations right in the text. For the full bibliographic data, the reader is referred to the "Works Cited" section at the end of the paper.

The form of the parenthetical reference in the text of the paper varies. Turabian, following the *Chicago Manual of Style*, uses a pattern of name, date, and page reference:

(White 1967, 1204)

The MLA format just uses a name and page reference:

(White 1204)

For MLA, if you are citing two or more works by one author, each work is numbered as follows:

(White 2:145)—i.e., the second item by White listed in the Works Cited.

If you have already referred to an author's name in the text of your paper, the citation will be only to the page number:

"White refers to this possibility (1204)."

■ ■ ■

The following is a brief presentation of both methods, using part of a paper I prepared myself. I would urge you, however, to obtain and adhere very closely to the style manual adopted by your own institution. These examples will not substitute for a full manual.

**Footnote System with
Traditional Title Page**

CHERNOBYL COLLEGE OF ECOLOGICAL CONCERN

ARE PROTESTANTS RESPONSIBLE FOR THE ENVIRONMENTAL
CRISIS?

A PAPER SUBMITTED FOR ECOLOGICAL ETHICS 305

BY

WILLIAM B. BADKE

LANGLEY, BRITISH COLUMBIA

SEPTEMBER, 1990

ARE PROTESTANTS RESPONSIBLE FOR THE ENVIRONMENTAL
CRISIS?

On March 10, 1967, historian Lynn White, Jr. dropped a bomb on the Protestant church. In an article entitled "The Historical Roots of our Ecologic Crisis," White argued that the Judeo-Christian ethic of dominion over nature was at the heart of western industrialization and has been the predominant motivation behind the West's cruel exploitation of the earth.[1]

While White's article has been reprinted extensively,[2] another, even more devestating, essay by Jackson Ice has been largely ignored. Ice listed five causes of the ecological crisis, all of them linked to Christianity and ultimately to Protestantism: Christian monotheism which, in triumphing over paganism,

---

[1]Lynn White, "The Historical Roots of our Ecologic Crisis," Science 155 (March 10, 1967): 1203-1207.

[2]See, for example, Garrett De Bell, ed. The Environmental Handbook (New York: Ballantine Books, 1970), 12-26; Wesley Granberg-Michaelson, Ecology and Life (Waco, Tex.: Word Books, 1988), 125-137; Francis A. Schaeffer, Pollution and the Death of Man (Wheaton, Ill.: Tyndale House Publishers, 1970), 97-115.

2

de-divinized Nature; the Christian view of dominion
which made Nature into "raw material to be subdued and
conquered;" an eschatology which anticipates the end of
Nature, followed by a new heavens and new earth; the
Christian idea of nonprogressive revelation, which
works against acceptance of new religious outlooks; and
the Protestant ethic, with its scheme of salvation,
which sanctioned Capitalism's greed for material gain.[3]

Are they right? Do White and Ice and the many
others who have blamed Protestantism for the world's
current environmental nightmare, have a case for
arguing that the Christian message is antagonistic to
the earth?

In order to evaluate these charges, it is
important to begin with the biblical message so that we
can determine whether the Christian Scriptures,
properly interpreted, do indeed sanction abuse of the
earth. Two passages are regularly cited by critics as
being at the heart of the problem: Genesis 1:28 and
Genesis 9:1-3.

In Genesis 1:28 we see what appears to be a clear

----

[3]Jackson Lee Ice, "The Ecological Crisis:
Radical Monotheism vs. Ethical Pantheism," Religion in
Life 44 (1975): 204-207.

WORKS CITED

De Bell, Garrett, ed. The Environmental Handbook. New
    York: Ballantine Books, 1970.

Granberg-Michaelson, Wesley. Ecology and Life. Waco,
    Tex.: Word Books, 1988.

Ice, Jackson Lee, "The Ecological Crisis: Radical
    Monotheism vs. Ethical Pantheism." Religion in
    Life 44:204-207.

Schaeffer, Francis A. Pollution and the Death of Man.
    Wheaton, Ill.: Tyndale House Publishers, 1970.

White, Lynn, "The Historical Roots of our Ecologic
    Crisis." Science 155:1203-1207.

Parenthetical Reference Systems

William B. Badke

Professor Sludge

Environmental ethics 305

Are Protestants Responsible for the Environmental
Crisis?

On March 10, 1967, historian Lynn White, Jr.
dropped a bomb on the Protestant church. In an article
entitled "The Historical Roots of our Ecologic Crisis,"
White argued that the Judeo-Christian ethic of dominion
over nature was at the heart of western
industrialization and has been the predominant
motivation behind the West's cruel exploitation of the
earth. (1203-1207).

While White's article has been reprinted
extensively (see De Bell 12-26; Granberg-Michaelson
125-137; Schaeffer 97-115), another, even more
devestating, essay by Jackson Ice has been largely
ignored. Ice listed five causes of the ecological
crisis, all of them linked to Christianity and
ultimately to Protestantism: Christian monotheism
which, in triumphing over paganism, de-divinized
Nature; the Christian view of dominion which made
Nature into "raw material to be subdued and conquered;"
an eschatology which anticipates the end of Nature,
followed by a new heavens and new earth; the Christian

idea of nonprogressive revelation, which works against acceptance of new religious outlooks; and the Protestant ethic, with its scheme of salvation, which sanctioned Capitalism's greed for material gain. (204-207).

Are they right? Do White and Ice and the many others who have blamed Protestantism for the world's current environmental nightmare, have a case for arguing that the Christian message is antagonistic to the earth?

In order to evaluate these charges, it is important to begin with the biblical message so that we can determine whether the Christian Scriptures, properly interpreted, do indeed sanction abuse of the earth. Two passages are regularly cited by critics as being at the heart of the problem: Genesis 1:28 and Genesis 9:1-3.

In Genesis 1:28 we see what appears to be a clear reference to a dominion mandate. Human beings were to subdue and fill the earth. If we are to evaluate the meaning of this verse, we must look at its context - the reference to humanity's creation in the "image of

WORKS CITED

De Bell, Garrett, ed. The Environmental Handbook. New
    York: Ballantine Books, 1970.

Granberg-Michaelson, Wesley. Ecology and Life. Waco,
    Tex.: Word Books, 1988.

Ice, Jackson Lee, "The Ecological Crisis: Radical
    Monotheism vs. Ethical Pantheism." Religion in
    Life 44 (1975): 204-207.

Schaeffer, Francis A. Pollution and the Death of Man.
    Wheaton, Ill.: Tyndale House Publishers, 1970.

White, Lynn, "The Historical Roots of our Ecologic
    Crisis." Science 155 (March 10, 1967): 1203-1207.

The Survivor's Guide to Library Research
was typeset by the
Photocomposition Department of Zondervan
Publishing House, Grand Rapids, Michigan
on a Mergenthaler Linotron 202/N.
Compositor: Susan A. Koppenol
Editor: Susan T. Lutz and Ed van der Maas

The text was set in 10 point Palatino, a face designed by
Hermann Zapf in Germany in 1948. Palatino is probably one of
the two most highly regarded typefaces of this century.

This book was printed by
Color House Graphics, Grand Rapids, Michigan.